BATH

For Gwen —
Have a wonderful
time in England.
With much love from
your Mr. W,

Scott

BATH

AN ARCHITECTURAL GUIDE

by

Charles Robertson

with an Introduction by

Jan Morris

Faber & Faber
Three Queen Square
London

First published in 1975
by Faber and Faber Limited
3 Queen Square London W.C.1

Printed in Great Britain
by Latimer Trend & Company Ltd
Plymouth

ISBN 0 571 10805 9 (Faber Paperback)
ISBN 0 571 10750 8 (hard bound edition)

*This book has been sponsored by the
Bath Festival and the City of Bath for
European Architectural Heritage Year*

Contents

Acknowledgments _page_ 7

Acknowledgments for Photographs 7

INTRODUCTION BY JAN MORRIS 9

HISTORICAL OUTLINE 27

A CHRONOLOGY OF BATH BUILDINGS, 1700–1900 34

PLANS

   1. Bath 39

   2. Bath, city centre 40

GAZETTEER 41

BATH ARCHITECTS 136

Short Bibliography 144

Index 145

Acknowledgments

Among the many people who have helped me with encouragement, advice and information, I would specially mention Peter Coard; Hugh Crallan whose unpublished chronological chart of Bath architects is invaluable; Alan Crozier-Cole whose architectural practice is in continuous descent from James Wilson and has been at the same address since 1846; Gerald Deacon; Lesley Green-Armytage; Francis Kelly; Peter Kidson; and Tony Mitchell who gave me a copy of his notes on Bath's Victorian buildings.

The responsibility for any errors is, of course, entirely mine.

C.J.R.

Acknowledgments for Photographs

Acknowledgments are due to the following for use
of photographs on the pages indicated

Aerofilms Ltd., 76–7

Bath Festival Society, 81 (top)

Bath Preservation Trust, 110

Brian G. Davis, Department of Architecture and Planning, Bath City Council, 50 (top), 53 (top), 57 (top), 63, 65 (top), 67 (foot), 80, 82 (top), 82 (foot), 93 (top), 114 (foot), 122 (foot)

E. L. Green-Armytage, 10, 12, 29, 32, 41, 42, 43, 48, 49 (top), 49 (foot), 52 (left), 52 (right), 56, 57 (foot), 58, 59 (top), 60 (top), 61 (top), 62 (left), 64 (foot), 65 (foot), 66 (top), 69, 71, 75, 78, 79, 83, 84, 90, 91, 92, 96, 97, 102, 103, 104, 105 (right), 107, 108 (top), 108–9, 111, 114 (top), 115, 120 (right), 121 (top), 121 (foot), 123, 127, 128, 129, 130 (right), 131 (top), 131 (foot)

Karl Jaeger, frontispiece

National Monuments Record, 60 (foot), 94 (top), 94 (foot), 95, 116

The Rev. Canon Maurice H. Ridgway, 45

Spa Director, Pump Room, Bath, 16, 46, 50 (foot), 51, 70, 100–1, 122 (top)

Stephanie Van Piere, 23, 53 (foot), 54, 55, 59 (foot), 61 (foot), 62 (right), 64 (top), 66 (foot), 67 (top), 72 (left), 72 (right), 73, 74, 81 (foot), 85, 86, 87 (left), 87 (right), 87 (foot), 88, 89, 93 (foot), 98, 99 (top), 99 (foot), 105 (left), 112, 113, 117, 118, 119, 120 (left), 124, 125, 126, 130 (left), 132 (top), 132 (foot), 133, 134

West Air Photography, 19

Introduction

by JAN MORRIS

THERE is one place in Bath, and one only, where I sometimes feel that I am standing in a great centre of the European tradition. It is on the south bank of the River Avon, and it is best reached by walking up the river path beside the sports grounds. One passes then beneath North Parade Bridge, and emerging from its shadowy underside, fringed with ivy and ornamented by enigmatic graffiti, one sees suddenly the heart of the city gracefully disposed about its river.

The scene is dominated by the sound of it, for here the river flows frothily over a weir, and its perpetual hiss and rumble always makes me think of elaborate water-gardens in France or Austria, or the rush of greater rivers through cities of nobler consequence. To the left rises the square pinnacled tower of Bath Abbey, English Perpendicular in fact, but looking from this vantage-point squatter and stronger than it really is, and Romanesque in posture. In front is the exquisite fancy of Pulteney Bridge, with the windows of its shops opened over the water like a lesser Ponte Vecchio, and the heads of a tourist or two eating cakes in the Venetian Coffee Shop. On the left, above the wide belvedere of Grand Parade, the bulk of the old Empire Hotel is an unmistakable hint of Carlsbad or Baden-Baden. Gardens run down to the water's edge, with a floral clock and deck-chairs in them, and through the water-noise one can hear the traffic on the street above, and perhaps the thump of a brass band. There is a steeple here, and a shallow dome there, and the brutal silhouette of a new tourist hotel shows inevitably above the bridge: and sometimes a man is fishing from a boat moored in the tumble of the weir, and there are pleasure launches or barges moored beside the towpath. It is a scene that suggests grandeur and decision—symphony orchestras, influential newspapers, stock exchanges, parliaments perhaps. It feels as though up there above the river stands one of the European fulcra, where art and religion, history and economics combine to create a universal artifact, common to us all.

This is an illusion. Bath has never been a great city at all, and stands provincially aloof to the European mainstream. That river, which suggests Seine or Volga, rises in the Cotswold slopes twenty miles above, debouches into the Severn estuary fifteen miles below, and Bath too is small, inconsequential and altogether English. It is true that the Romans, exploiting the hot springs of this valley, made Aquae Sulis one of the best-known of their colonial spas, and that the medieval Abbey, like all the great English churches, grew up in close communion with its peers across the Channel. But Bath itself, Bath of the Georgian splendours, Bath of the golden stones and the Pump Room minuet, the Bath that Jane Austen knew and loathed, that Sheridan eloped from, that Gainsborough learnt his art in, that Clive, Nelson, Pope and Mrs. Thrale retreated to—Bath of the Bath buns and the Bath chairs, Bath of the dowagers, Bath that greets the visitor terraced and enticing as the train swings into Spa Station down Brunel's line from Paddington—the Bath of the persistent legend is a Somerset borough of

THE CIRCUS

the middle rank, rather bigger than Annecy, say, about the size of Delft. Its contacts with the greater world have been frequent, but tangential. A thousand years ago the first coronation of a King of all England took place in Bath, but since then the monarchs, the presidents and the premiers have come here only for pleasure, escape or lesser ceremony—an emperor in exile, a queen in search of pregnancy, a prime minister electioneering, a king comforting the victims of war.

Modern Bath is not, like those greater archetypes, an organic kind of city. Though it has existed on this site for nearly 2,000 years, the city we now know is more or less a fluke. For twelve centuries after the departure of the Romans it was an ordinary country town, distinguished from a thousand others only by the presence of the springs, and it was a sudden flare of fashion and fortuitous genius that made it, in the eighteenth century, a city *sui generis*. For forty or fifty years, perhaps, Bath was the most fashionable resort in England, and almost everything unique about it was created then, for a particular local purpose, mostly by local men. The publicists call it Bath, the Georgian City, but Georgian Bath was hardly more than a flash-in-the-pan—a craze, a passing enthusiasm, which soon petered out as crazes do, leaving the city to potter on once more as a bourgeois West Country town, known to the world chiefly for its Roman past and its literary associations, and inhabited in the popular fancy almost entirely by retired valetudinarians.

Yet that transient flowering of fashion has left behind it one of the loveliest cities in the world, ironically preserved by its loss of glory. This is not, like Venice or Vienna, the capital of a vanished empire, or the seat of a discredited dynasty. One cannot mourn here forgotten kings, ruined bankers, defeated marshals. Bath's function was never very significant. People came here first to cure their agues, and then to have fun. There is nothing to be sad about, as we survey Bath's towers and trees across the river. The view may be evocative, but it is not in the least disturbing, for it is only a suggestion anyway, just as the bright genius of Bath is hardly more than a beautiful display, the whim or flourish of an era.

Walk on a little further, past the new flood gate, up the winding stone staircase beside the bridge; and on the road above you will find no horseback monuments of Hapsburg or Bernadotte, only agreeable little shops, and a closer view of the tourists in the coffee shop, on their second cream slice by now, and petunias in wire baskets, and the piano showroom of Messrs. Duck, Son and Pinker, and the gateway to the covered market behind the Guildhall, where Mr. Bennett is licensed to sell Woodcock, Snipe and Venison, and Mrs. Reason offers her delectable and home-cooked Pickled Pork.

But if Power is not an attribute of Bath, Authority distinctly is—not the authority of political regimes, but the authority of manners. It is by no means a sanctimonious city: nineteenth-century Bath toughs were notorious, and Saturday night in Broad Street can still be a rumbustious celebration. It gives, though, an instant impression of *order*. Its very shape is logical. Its true centre, the Abbey churchyard, stands on the site of the original Roman temple, above the hot springs themselves. Around it in a circle lies the medieval city, within the circuit of its mostly vanished walls, and spreading away in all directions, up the Lansdown slopes to the north, up Bathwick, Widcombe and Lyncombe Hills to the south, along the line of the river east and west, Georgian, Victorian and twentieth-century Bath extends itself in terraces, crescents and respectable estates. It is a compact and manageable place. It has few sprawling suburbs, and its patterns are straightforward and easy to grasp.

The Romans, of course, brought their own method here, and the plan of their Bath, now mostly buried under the city streets, seems to have been functional to a degree, with its oblong temple precinct and its systematic bathing establishment, elegantly disposed about the shrine to Sul-Minerva, patron goddess of the site. But it was the eighteenth century which, deliberately copying Roman precedents, made Bath synonymous with rational design and integrated manners. The fashionable world then adopted the spa as a gambling centre, and London society flocked to its tables, bringing their vices with them: but the enlightened if ludicrous major-domo Richard Nash, a fastidious Welsh opportunist, so disciplined them into more reasonable behaviour that his Bath set the style of an age, and permanently affected the English balance of life. Under his supervision society restrained itself, tamed its horse-squires, brought its duchesses down to earth, until the middle and upper classes actually danced with one another, and the old hierarchy was discredited for good.

'Beau' Nash's autocracy of deportment was to be miraculously translated into the stone serenity that is the architectural glory of Bath. The city's great builders of the eighteenth century were frankly speculators, spotting and satisfying a market—most of their houses were lodging houses, to be let to families visiting Bath for the season. But their progenitor, John Wood the elder, was an antiquarian too, and in building his squares and terraces he drew upon

BATH STREET

older inspirations—on the Roman example, on the Palladian disciplines, even some suggest upon ancient schemes of pre-history, with their astronomically exact circles of stone, and their arcane but determined intentions. Georgian Bath became a city of right angles or gentle curves, uniform heights, uniform materials, built into its hillsides with a Classical assurance, and sometimes even managing to look, in its long unbroken expanses of column and window, Druidically reticent. Nothing could be at once more controlled and more allusive than Wood's celebrated Circus, a perfect circle with three exits, its thirty-three houses decorated with a frieze of artistic, scientific and occupational symbols, lyres, masonic tools, the Aesculapian staff: and from the air Georgian Bath looks, with its geometric patterning, the perfect diagram of civic system.

Even the florid Victorians were restrained by the reasonableness of Bath, and in their passage through the city expressed themselves classically. The Kennet and Avon Canal, duckhaunted and lily-floated now, once the highway of coal barges and lumber-scows, passed with a calm resolution through the southern part of the city, with its fine stone locks and its truly Roman passage beneath the structure of its own headquarters, Cleveland House—where a trapdoor in the floor, we are told, allowed the administrators to pass their instructions directly into the grimy hands of the bargees sweating beneath. When I. K. Brunel drove his broad-gauge track so magnificently down the Thames Valley, coming to Bath he did as the Romans did, building his bridges and culverts and tunnels in a grandeur of fine-dressed stone, sweeping gloriously beside the river, and only pausing with the waywardness of genius to build his Bath Spa Station in a sort of castellated Tudor.

Today Bath's authority is of a weaker kind, and expresses itself chiefly in mock-Georgian buildings of a flaccid inoffensiveness. Occasionally, though, one sees in the city streets, or waiting in the station forecourt, big black limousines with flagstaffs on their bonnets, driven by chauffeurs of faintly military mien, and stepped into, when the train comes in or the luncheon is over, by men of unmistakable command. You may suppose them to be successors in some sort to the old Beau, supervisors of the city manners: but no, they are the senior bureaucrats and occasional Admirals of the Navy Department, several of whose branches settled in Bath for safety's sake during the war, and have been here ever since. They do impose order of a kind on Bath, though, for they provide the city's biggest industry, and give to their scattered premises, from the Empire Hotel which is their headquarters to the massed huts and car parks of Foxhill, a recognizably tight-lipped air. What is more, they have actually brought to Bath, if only in ellipsis, a true element of power: for it is here in the Georgian city of reason that the Royal Navy designs its nuclear submarines, which prowl the oceans perpetually on our behalf, and can obliterate almost anyone almost anywhere.

But there, no city could be much less warlike than Bath, and the Vice-Admiral who generally heads the Bath naval establishment is always a popular figure at Bath civic functions, addressing Rotary Clubs or presenting prizes. Anyway Bath depends far less upon its achievements than its people. Nuclear submarines apart, Bath has discovered a new planet (Uranus), devised a new shorthand (Pitman's), invented a new biscuit (Bath Olivers), fostered a masterpiece (*Tom Jones*), given its name to a bun and an invalid chair; but in general the city prides itself much more upon its illustrious visitors. Most celebrated Britons come to Bath at one time or another, and many distinguished foreigners too, but they have seldom *done* much in Bath—they have simply been there. The houses of Bath burgeon with plaques recording the residence of writers and admirals, empire builders and politicians, but often they only spent a season there in rented lodgings, recuperating for another battle, or correcting proofs.

Never mind, each left his trace behind him, however shadowy, and added a little to the mystique. I see them often, those elusive shades, as I wander the city. Miss Austen looks a little disgruntled as she picks her way between the puddles towards the circulating library. Lord Nelson looks a little wan as he opens his window in Pierrepont Street to see how the wind blows. Livingstone is pursued by admirers when he returns to No. 13, Royal Crescent, from his lecture at the Mineral Water Hospital. The great Duchess of Queensberry gasps, bursts into laughter and apologizes when Beau Nash tears her point lace apron from her waist and throws it to the ladies' maids. Pope limps through the gardens of Prior Park with his host, the Bath entrepreneur Ralph Allen, whose quarries provided the stone of Bath, and whose mansion magnificently surveys it. Sir Isaac Pitman scrupulously supervises the lettering, in his own phonetic script, on his new PRINTIN OFIS. Pepys taps his feet to the music of the peripatetic Bath fiddlers—'as good as ever I heard in London almost, or anywhere: 5s'. Wolfe, at his lodgings in Trim Street, opens the letter from London which will send him to victory and death at Quebec. The exiled Emperor of Ethiopia, bolt upright in silken cloak, disappears like a wraith on the morning train to Paddington.

They come and go to this day, celebrities of every category, still to be seen spooning the Raspberry Syllabub at Popjoy's, or nosing in hired Daimlers around the Lansdown terraces. Bath views them with pleasure, but with detachment. There will always be others, and any-way the citizens of Bath, like retainers at some princely household, keep their own character, live their own lives, unaffected by the passing of the great. More than most of the world's cities, Bath is familiar with fame, but in a very English way it remains in its deepest essence an ordinary provincial town: and though I know of few cities less anthropomorphic in character, so that I am never tempted to call Bath 'she', or give the place human qualities of its own, still it depends for its true flavour not upon those commemorative plaques or imaginary shades, but upon its own inhabitants.

Though Bath is magnificent, you will soon find that it is more homely than proud, its personality being at odds with its appearance. This is because the Bathonian is essentially a countryman still. The Bath dialect is roundly Somerset. The Bath face is unmistakably West Country, plump, genial. Nearly everyone remarks upon the gentle Bath manners—not exactly graceful, but nearly always kind. Bath is well-stocked with country things, in from the country that day, Mendip cheeses, Somerset butters, wholemeal breads from Priston Mill, rough ciders, Cotswold vegetables. Even in the central parts of the city kitchen gardens flourish, horses, cows and sometimes even sheep graze. It is only twelve miles down the road to Bristol, that gateway to the Americas, but Bath feels a thousand miles from the sea and its affairs, and is essentially a country town still, where the green hills show at the end of the street, and the country people buy their tights at Marks and Spencer's.

Bath looks so patrician that many visitors suppose it to be socially glittering still, as it was when, during the brief kingdom of Beau Nash, society preferred his court to that of the King of England. It looks, after all, like a city of great town houses, attended by cottage streets and council flats for the domestics. But again it is illusion. Grand people live in Bath, people with butlers, people with titles, people with Rolls Royces—people with shoe factories, or useful speculative properties in South London, or yachts in the Aegean. But they do not form a ruling caste, or even make one Bath address much better than another (though some of them would dearly like to). If you perambulate the city in the evening, peering through the half-drawn blinds and inspecting the names on doorbells, you will probably wonder what sort of people live in these parts: the answer must be—no sort. Bath still has its old-school trades-people, kindly maiden ladies in haberdashery, or elderly white-coated grocers who ask if they may deliver the cheeses, Madam, and there is to the very courtesy of its populace a faint suggestion of old precedences: but in fact the city is a social *mélange*, all its classes jumbled, none of its addresses exclusive, hippy beside general, writer below property tycoon.

There are the officials of the Navy Department, of course, whose senior officials form perhaps the most tightly knit community of Bath, and who tend to live in the country out-side, or in the villa-country of the southern slopes. There is the usual layer of provincial worthies, the solicitors, the doctors, the businessmen and their wives who provide the muni-cipal conscience, and covet the municipal perquisites, in any such town. Retired people tradi-tionally come to Bath: once they were likely to be rich West Indian planters, or East India merchants, and were buried beneath florid inscriptions in the Abbey, now they are usually pensioned and obscure, live among college crests or Ashanti shields in upstairs flats, and are interred in gloomy cemeteries.

There is a semi-academic community, too, that emanates from Bath's University of Technology, and is inclined to inhabit bare rooms with Japanese lanterns and adjustable book-shelves—and a bearded and scrawny kind of hippy community which has made Bath a stopping place on the pilgrim routes to Glastonbury and St. Ives—and a growing number of people who have come to paint, write, sculpt and meditate in Bath—and lots of teachers from Bath's innumerable schools—and all the shopkeepers, of course, and the artisans, and the workers in Bath's light industries, who provide the true constants of Bath, whose fathers and grandfathers lived in the street before them, and who feel as though they have remained totally unaffected, cheerfully grinning from their cranes, taking tea breaks on the front stairs, or explaining why it can't be done, come rain or shine, climax or decay, since they took over the place from the Romans.

In 1974 squatters moved into an empty house in the Royal Crescent, the haughtiest of the Bath terraces, and settled there making mildly revolutionary gestures. Some of the neigh-bours thought this the beginning of the end, but in fact the revolution came to Bath long ago. Occasionally, it is true, I do imagine its crescents peeling and unkempt under a philistine dictatorship, or forcibly converted into workers' holiday homes, and I seem to see the last of the admirals' widows scrubbing the floors of ideological museums, and those dear old grocers' assistants surreptitiously delivering black market butter to the back doors of lifelong customers. But I suspect it will never happen, for already the old structure is shattered, those aristocratic front doors are mostly no more than apartment block entrances, and the old styles linger on not as expressions of political form or social rigidity, but simply out of good country manners.

The hot springs of Bath, which gush from the ground at a temperature of 120 degrees Fahrenheit, are the *raison d'être* of Bath. To understand what this means, one has only to go down to the Roman Baths, sunken among their perambulatories beside the Abbey, and enter the big bronze doors behind which the springs of Aquae Sulis still issue from the rock. By any standards of travel this is a profoundly moving experience, for men have been restoring themselves with these waters without a break for nearly two thousand years. THIS HOT SPRING USED BY THE ROMANS, says an inscription above the door, HAS BEEN FROM TIME IMMEMORIAL THE PRINCIPAL SOURCE OF THE HEALTH-GIVING WATERS OF BATH. The air is hot and clammy in there, the steam billows, but there is to that dark grotto a wonderful suggestion not merely of age, or continuity, but of *solace*.

THE ROMAN BATHS, the Great Bath

Solace, in one form or another, is the truest purpose of Bath. Legend says that Prince Bladud, a hazy prince of the Britons, discovered the healing properties of the Bath springs when his leprous swine wallowed in the mud of this valley. Certainly the Romans soon discovered both the pleasures and the cures of the waters, and Aquae Sulis became a health resort well known throughout the western Empire. Though the baths themselves fell into ruin under the Saxons, and were not excavated until the nineteenth century, the springs were never forgotten: throughout the centuries of Bath's obscurity people drank and bathed in them—Charles II came in 1677, James II in 1687. One of Bath's most popular souvenirs is a print of the baths in 1675, a Hogarthian scene of squalor and vivacity, men, women and children all in the pool together, some naked, some ridiculously clothed, floating on their backs, splashing each other, diving off the conduit, while from the windows of the surrounding houses, from the balconies, all around the balustrade, the yokels of the city idly gawk. 'Methink', wrote Pepys in 1668, 'it cannot be clean to go so many bodies together in the same water.'

Directly from the waters, too, sprang the eighteenth-century climax of Bath, though now the search for bodily health or vigour was diversified into a quest for pleasure. Bath was a place for gambling and dalliance, promenade and theatre, as well as a spa. Beau Nash was one of the sponsors of the Mineral Water Hospital, but he was far more concerned with the social life of Bath than its medical system, and so were most of his clients. Theirs was a solace of the spirit, and today too, though the Royal National Hospital for Rheumatic Diseases still pipes the waters to its treatment rooms, though Bath is full of prosperous doctors, and though most self-respecting visitors to the Pump Room take a dubious sip from the conduit ('wery strong flavour o' warm flat-irons', Sam Weller thought), still the best purpose of the modern city is simply to give delight.

Like most pleasure-cities, Bath can be uncommonly displeasing, mostly by contrast. When the weather is wrong, or the mood jars, even the splendours of the place go sour. Then the honey-gold turns to grey, the hills look drab and lifeless, the young people seem to disappear from the streets, and Bath seems despondently sunk in its muggy valley—its sulphurous pit, as Pope called it. It can be a claustrophobic city: the hot springs underground, perhaps, give it a stifling feeling, and the orderly ranks of its terraces can look heartless and impersonal, standing there door by door in the drizzle.

But catch the right day, the right wind, and then Bath can be the very happiest city in England. Then the crescents and squares look no longer regimented, but benign and comradely. Then the grey deserts the stone, and the gold creeps back. The average age of the populace seems to drop by twenty years or so, the tables outside the pubs are full and lively, long skirts swish down Milsom Street, guitar music sounds from the upstairs pads of Park Street. Bath seems full of flowers then, and the little pedestrian alleys in the city centre are bright with fruit, trendy clothes and *Private Eye*, and on the green below the Royal Crescent the small boys of the Jamaican community set up their stumps and play deft and hilarious cricket in the sun.

Then the order of the place becomes not an imposition, but a liberation. As the black of a dinner-jacket sets off the bright colours of a dress, so the squares, crescents, quadrangles and circles of Bath provide a grand geometric stage for the flow of life that passes through it. Against such an imperturbable background, almost anything goes better: a military tattoo, a car rally, an outdoor performance of Molière, cricket, throwing frisbees, eating pork pies in pub gardens—Bath has the gift of heightening all activities, and giving an unexpected beauty to everyday affairs. If I am having trouble with a recalcitrant paragraph, I simply go outside and wander through the town for half an hour: and the proportions of the place, the green interventions, the honey-stone and the gentle faces, soon put my adjectives in order, and calm my restless cadences.

B

This recuperative power resides partly in the manner of Bath—a smooth, bedside manner that is set by its Georgian dominants. It is a densely built city—no more than a couple of miles across, and rounded—and like many of the greatest architectural ensembles, like the cities of inner Spain, or the prairie clusters of the American West, its best parts have an oddly portable feel to them. So dexterously fitted are their sections to one another, so organically embedded in their setting, that one feels they could be prised *in toto* from their environment, and lifted for closer examination. All around the countryside shows, wherever you look, and this green frame accentuates the easy unity of Bath, too, as the sea undeniably gives extra point to an island.

Because of the narrow scale, the beauty of Georgian Bath depends heavily upon perspective. Depth and vista are essential to these buildings, and no city is more vulnerable to the distortion of the telephoto lense. Built on flat ground, Bath would lose half its fascination: its architectural emphasis is mostly horizontal, and the rolling hills around, the gradual slope towards the river valley, the rich green trees of park and garden, provide the necessary uprights. But there is no hint of *trompe l'oeil* to the great buildings of Bath. They are rational, gentlemanly, straightforward buildings, thoroughly English, whose effects are achieved not by deceit, but by relationships.

One of the delights of Bath is the shift of its planes, building against building, street behind street, as though some master producer is juggling with his stage sets. Because it is not truly a great city, powerful of meaning or intent, the pace of this architectural parade can be light-hearted. One does not wish to hurry a Paris or an Edinburgh, solemn as they are with memories of faith and history, or even a New York, where humanity itself seems to have reached some kind of frenzied apotheosis. But Bath is only for fun, and anyway is so small that one can always come round a second time, so that for myself, though I love to walk about the city, I think it displays itself best of all from the windows of a slowly moving car. Then the surprises and entertainments of the place, which are essentially frivolous, move at the right cheerful pace. The smooth lines of the city masonry glide along un-jogged, the crescents slide by with the proper sensuous motion, and the serendipities of Bath fall thick and fast.

Of these the most celebrated occurs at the end of Brock Street, on the lower slope of Lansdown. It is among the most famous of architectural surprises, and provides one of the happiest moments of European sight-seeing. I experience it myself a couple of hundred times a year, but I never tire of it. This Bath moment especially is best observed by car, and I like to do it with the roof open and something blithe and brilliant on the tape—Mozart, Mendelssohn, or Astaire singing Cole Porter. Then I swing exuberantly around the Circus, beneath the marvellous centre-piece of planes (cocking a snook as I go at those grim purists who would chop them down for architecture's sake), and head down the short, straight link road called Brock Street. I pretend I have never been there before, and for visual reasons drive slap down the middle of the street. At the end there seems to be a vacancy—cloud, trees, a snatch of green, the corner of a large house protruding slightly in the middle distance, a transverse terrace beyond. Is it a park? Is it a football ground? Is it a demolition site? The plan gives nothing away; the vacancy remains vacant; only that sense of impending space grows as I approach the end of the road; and then, narrowly avoiding the Mini which, in a less exuberant condition, emerges aghast from Church Street, I top the barely perceptible rise, ease myself around the corner, and find before me one of the most splendid *tours de force* of European design, the Royal Crescent.

THE ROYAL CRESCENT from the air, with Brock Street and the Circus

It lies there in a shallow arc, its wide lawns running away beyond the ha-ha down the hill below, and all is suddenly space, and green, and leisure. Though the Crescent is architecture on a truly palatial scale, and reminds many people of Versailles, to me it suggests far more pungently the seaside. It is like the grandest of all rows of seaside villas, standing on a promenade before a sea of grass: the children bathe on the green below, the householders walk their dogs along the beach, and the sign that enjoins No Organized Games is merely a delicate way of saying that if you are looking for What The Butler Saw, try the pier. I have seen visitors stopped in their tracks as, turning that same corner of Brock Street, they have discovered this glorious scene in front of them: and the look of astonished delight upon their faces is just the look the holiday-makers have when, tumbling from the train and walking down Beach Street from the station, they have reached the esplanade that is their destination, and see the sands, all balloons, whelks and motor-boat trips, there in the sun before them.

No *trompe l'oeil*: but if the charm of Bath is not deceptive, it is unexpectedly intricate. It relies upon contrast, for all among those splendid set-pieces, wedged in here and there, corners of quirk or curiosity provide a filigree. Narrow steps and alleys lead the eye to greater spectacles; railings, brackets, details of stone and iron-work throw into grander relief the classical frontages behind; artisan cottages correct the scale of things; grace-notes relieve the splendour. Symmetries are broken. Incongruities occur. Much of this complicated sub-Bath, this civic undergrowth, has lately been destroyed, sometimes for good social reasons, more often because of planners' naïvety, developers' greed and architects' sterility. Just enough remains to preserve the flavour. There are enclaves of petty Georgian, like Beaufort Square, behind the Theatre Royal, which possesses a crooked, almost edible allure, as though all its little houses are made of pastry. There are follies, like Beckford's Tower on Lansdown Hill, or Allen's Sham Castle across the valley. There are streets like Walcot Street, beside the river, which begins with a bang in the jolly Hat and Feather, ends in a whimper with the hapless new Beaufort Hotel, but contains in its short length a heady jumble of chapels, terraces, junk shops, hippie hang-outs, derelict gardens, old steps, gates that go nowhere, cul-de-sacs, an arcaded corn market, a green graveyard—the whole made fragrant by the smell of new bread from the Red House Bakery and raw meat from the cold storage depot, and sneeringly overlooked by the immense curve of the Paragon above.

Take Lansdown Crescent, which stands regally on the upper Lansdown slopes, white-painted and festively illuminated by its own wrought-iron gate lamps. Lansdown has more panache than the Royal Crescent, with its undulating double curves and its rising and falling ground, but it is still very magnificent, and stylishly inhabited. Butlers and judges are to be found in these fine houses, rich manufacturers, bankers' widows, art historians. One house is furnished basement to attic entirely in the Georgian mode, and to the house once inhabited by the mystic Francis Younghusband a hardly less visionary American has brought a new kind of civilized living to Bath, part Japanese, part Manhattan, with a square sunken bath in the Roman kind, and a carpeted, sun-decked penthouse of exquisite indulgence.

Yet this famous crescent is embedded in crinklier matter. Directly in front of those magnificent houses, an unkempt meadow tumbles steeply down the escarpment, infested by nettles and thistles, and grazed by horses, heifers, sometimes even sheep. Directly behind them, a gnome-like settlement flourishes. There are converted stables with creepers winding round their drain-pipes, and little cobbled yards with children's tricycles in them, and ivy-locked garden gates, and damp dead-end passages, and apple-trees, and motor-scooters in sheds, and summer-houses through whose windows, impenitently peering, one may discover half-completed water-colours, animal skulls, old pianos or book-presses. It is like another country back there, or a colony of churls and craftsmen in the purlieus of a princely court.

Or consider the piazetta at the heart of Bath—the Abbey Churchyard, site of the altar of Sul-Minerva, which one best enters under the colonnade from Stall Street. This lies in the middle of Bath's down-town circumstance, such as it is. One side of the little square is formed by the façade of the Pump Room, another consists of eighteenth-century shops, and the end is blocked by the imposing west front of the Abbey, with its huge carved door and its angels tumbling up and down their ladders to heaven.

It is quite a noble arrangement, but if the frame is monumental, the scene is miniature—like a toy piazza. On a summer day its benches are usually crowded with tourists, shoppers and idlers. A little bar is set up in the shadow of the colonnade, with sun-shades and rows of bottles, and groups of very foreign visitors wander in and out of the Pump Room doors, in and out of the dark Abbey, gazing into the souvenir shops or wondering whether to commission a plaque of their own family arms from Mr. Howe on the corner. It is, though, fundamentally a domestic scene. The Abbey front towers above it all, but still there are prams about, and housewives gossiping over their coffee. You can have your hair done here, or order a pair of spectacles, and above the premises of Alfred Shore and Sons ('Distinction in Dress Shoes') one may sometimes see Mr. Greenwood the dentist actually at his drill. Napoleon called St Mark's Square the finest drawing-room in Europe, but the Abbey Churchyard is no more than the most agreeable parlour in England, a little place, an intimate place, a place to chat or sew in, or decide what to get for supper.

There is a poignancy to this diminutive side of Bath, or if not a poignancy, a wistfulness. Come inside the Pump Room, now. The Pump Room Trio is performing, as it does every weekday morning, and the handsome room is full of visitors, drinking fairly muddy coffee, sampling the spa water from the tap in the bay window, or looking down to the water of the King's Bath outside. Kindly waitresses bustle about, the tall Tompion clock ticks away against the wall, Beau Nash stares superciliously from his statue in its niche. The musicians play on stage behind a palisade of geraniums, potted palms on a balcony above their heads, and I often go down there to enjoy their company, correcting a manuscript over my coffee, or just observing the scene. It is not only that they play *Rosemarie*, *Oklahoma* or *Perchance to Dream* with a splendid enthusiasm: it is also because they seem to represent a culture that has almost died—a lost, innocent culture, fitfully and nostalgically surviving here. They must be almost the last café trio still performing in Great Britain; I take many visitors to hear them, and they often make a deeper impression than the Roman Baths.

This is a melancholy pleasure, but then some of Bath's fascination *is* melancholy. Before the Second World War it was a much sadder place than it is now, and old photographs show it drab, blackened and down-at-heel, even its prodigies looking sadly neglected, and its detail obscured with dirt and excrescences. But even today, though most of it is spick and span, it often has a sadness to it. People analyse this in different ways. Some think it is just nostalgia for the eighteenth century, which seems so close in Bath, but is really so far away. Some put it down to the climate, which can be horrid. Some again are depressed by the introspective feel of the place, or are enervated by the uniformity of its stone. Some dislike its museum feeling, some are desolated by its changes, and one or two I have met are placed at a particular disadvantage by their distaste for Georgian architecture.

I myself attribute the sensation to an unfulfilment in Bath. Since the end of the eighteenth century, and the departure of the fashionable to newer and racier resorts, Bath has never recaptured its purpose—or rather, the particular purpose that the Georgians gave it, and for which their glories were designed. Bath is only a bourgeois Somerset town, dressed like a capital: a city built for art and pleasure, trying to be a Regional Shopping Centre. There are attempts to make it more—the Festival of the Arts, the Arts Workshop, the Bath Preservation Trust, the American Museum. Bath has many devoted amateurs, and several well-intentioned patrons. The City Fathers, though, are reluctant to accept its hedonist place in the world, so that it remains something of a façade. Its palaces are not palaces, only blocks of flats. Its Abbey is only a parish church. Its Festival happens once a year, and when it is over the performers and choreographers, arrangers and composers disperse again, leaving the city to the Pump Room Trio and the electronic organ in the Parade Gardens.

The backs of Bath buildings are very revealing. A few of the swankiest terraces are grand behind too, but for the most part Bath's builders did not much care about rear elevations, and successive improvers and developers have stuck their additions haphazard on the back walls, giving half Bath a hodge-podge, job-lot look which I particularly like. The back of Marlborough Buildings offers one such spectacle. This is a large range of terrace houses, built speculatively in the late 1780s. From the front it looks decorous, especially No. 9 (where I live). From the back it looks an enthralling muddle. There are allotment gardens back there, and if you stroll among their beans and chrysanthemums, looking up to the massive wall of masonry above, the effect is troglodytic. It is as though a natural rock-face stands there, pitted with the thousand caves and burrows that are its windows. There are thirty-three houses in the row, and from the back all look different. Some have six floors, some five. Some are impeccably maintained, some look like slums. Their windows are splodged or hacked almost indeterminately across the cliff, and there are balconies stuck on here and there, and outhouses, and jutting alcoves like Turkish *mahrabiyas*, and sham windows here, and blocked doors there, and racks for flower-boxes, and washing-lines, and sometimes the curtains look richly velvet, and sometimes they appear to consist of a couple of discarded blankets strung up on cord.

In another city those little private havens would be full of purpose, and Marlborough Buildings does of course house its quota of business people, civil servants, students, even a writer or two. But Bath lacks the tautness of a truly functional city, a city that fits its own buildings, and when I stroll back there in the evening I often think what a melancholy diffusion of energy that cliff face represents. How many of those windows, I think, represent not a purpose, but a lack of it! Widows, childless divorcees, elderly unmarried ladies, dilettantes, pensioners, the retired—Bath is full of lonely people without occupations, counting the days until their grandchildren come to call, killing the evening with television, gin or marijuana, plotting another bridge party, waiting for Bingo, or setting off down the hill for an hour with the Pump Room Trio. Every city has its share of the purposeless, but by the nature of things Bath has more than most, and the saddest of the bell-push names, I think, are those whose faded pride lives on in a polished but almost indecipherable brass plate, or a visiting card engraved in the deep copper-plate of long ago.

This human emptiness has its physical counter-part too. If much of Bath is newly restored, much is hang-dog still. There are houses never rebuilt since the blitz, or awaiting, year after year, planning permission or builders' cash. There are abandoned churches up for sale. Through the cracks of stately flagstones tufts of grass spring through, and sometimes the corner of a garden, the elbow of an alley, is choked with creeper and bramble, as though a civilization has retreated here, and the weeds are taking over. It is another illusion of course

THE PUMP ROOM, ceiling of Concert Room

—Bath is in better shape than it has been for many decades: but still the tristesse is real, in this city that is too splendid for itself, and often it creeps through Bath in the late afternoon, or one awakes to find it hanging over the city like a cloud, deadening the repartee of the milk-man, and sending many of the old ladies, I suspect, sensibly back to bed again.

I am thinking chiefly of public Bath, prodigy Bath, those districts of the city that were specifically built for its eighteenth-century climax. Elsewhere, of course, the older, more modest functions of the town survive as always, and all the structure of an English country borough has been handed down undisturbed from the Middle Ages. One pleasant way to sense this other Bath, I think, is to desert the Lansdown slopes and the city centre, where the tourists swarm, and cross the river, the railway and the canal to the hills of the southern side. Here is another city altogether, hardly less beautiful in its less showy way, and closer perhaps to the inner spirit of the place, which has resisted so many shifts of fortune, and remains essentially quiet and countrified.

There are terraces over there, and cottages, and new housing estates, and there used to be some fairly rugged slums, but it is above all villa country on the slopes of the southern hills. Scattered through the trees towards Claverton scores of half-Italianate, half-Regency villas stand among their gardens, some luxurious, some modest, all very private. They are lived in by families, most of them, not divided into flats, and they retain a sprightly and comfortable air. They are not show houses. They are real. Children play in their gardens, and the pater-familias drives home from the office in his Rover. Here one realizes the true social condition of Bath: an unexceptionable country town beneath it all, with its own private pedigree of burgher, tradesmen and labourer, its own civic preoccupations, its own narrow coteries and rivalries, come legionary, come Beau.

Only the presence of lost genius makes it special, elevating it to a status far above itself, and the best place of all, I think, to enjoy this pungent and ironic state of affairs, where the ordinary meets the superb, the parochial touches the international, is at Widcombe, in the heart of the villa country. This is one of those ancient country hamlets which have been absorbed into the fabric of the city, and it is recognizably a village still, with its church, its manor house and its village war memorial. Widcombe feels immensely old, and stable in a rural way, as though it recognizes deep in its stones and roots that the business of life is living itself.

Beside the church a lane leads steeply up the hill. It meanders on for a couple of hundred yards, and then comes to a halt at an iron gate beside some cottages. To my mind this is the most Bathonian place in Bath, truer by far to the city's spirit than that metropolitan view beside the river, and more telling than any contrived delight of the Lansdown crescents. The cottages beside you are true country cottages, *rus in urbe*, with moss-grown steps and cherished vegetable gardens. Green fields rise all about, giving the dell a properly nooky feel, and through the gates one may see a gamekeeper's cottage, and a sedgy lake with swans, ducks and moorhens in it.

It is a gentle scene, part country, part town, and unpretentiously assured: but beyond the lake there stands something very different—the exquisite little Palladian bridge, roofed and pillared, built long ago for the delectation of Ralph Allen, when he walked with his guests in his mansion high above. It is a little golden structure, all by itself in the green, which stands there with an air of mock naivety, but which speaks of Rome and Vicenza, Pope and Goldsmith, minuets and royal visits, and all the heady ideas, idioms and experiences which have, down the centuries, brought to this modest English town a fantasy of greatness, and by fostering it with such grace, fun and harmony, made the illusion true.

General Wolfe's House and 'Trim Bridge', Trim Street

Historical Outline

by CHARLES ROBERTSON

BATH has a continuous history of at least nineteen hundred years, and is rightly regarded as one of the marvels of Europe's architectural heritage; so that it is perhaps a surprise to find how little of what one sees today predates the eighteenth century. There are of course the Roman Baths, the finest Roman remains in Britain, which survived by being buried deep beneath the city; and the Abbey church, very late Gothic, begun in its present form in 1500 and incomplete at the dissolution. Almost everything else was swept away by the eighteenth-century developments. There is, of course, the town plan. The line of the western half of the city walls can quite easily be traced on a modern map simply by following the street names: clockwise from the South Gate at the north end of Southgate Street along Lower Borough Walls and Westgate Buildings (the West Gate was at the corner with Westgate Street) up to the Sawclose, earlier called the Timber Green, and turning right along the straight line of Upper Borough Walls (where a much-restored fragment of the wall survives) to the North Gate at the south end of the present Northgate Street. The eastern half of the walls is less easy to trace, but it roughly followed the line of the two Orchard Streets and Terrace Walk before turning north-west across the land now occupied by the Empire Hotel and the Market. Within the area thus enclosed the positions, and the names, of some sites survive: Stall Street, Cheap Street, Bridewell Lane, High Street, Bilberry Lane, Abbey Green, St. John's Hospital, the Hot and Cross Baths. But above ground there is very little of significance before 1700; Hetling House, now Abbey Church House and of about 1570, is the best survival of its time but has been entirely rebuilt. Inside is a fine chimney-piece. The 'Grapes' in Westgate Street has a good seventeenth-century ceiling. Most remarkable is the total disappearance of all the city's medieval parish churches. There were four of these within the walls: St. Mary's near the North Gate, St. Michael's near the West Gate, St. James's near the South Gate, and St. Mary de Stalles right at the centre of the little city. Even the sites have gone, although St. James's did not finally give way to Woolworth's until 1955.

Medieval Bath seems tiny by modern standards—the total area enclosed by the walls was only twenty-three acres—but it was evidently flourishing and prosperous. There was the Abbey, more correctly called the Priory, which was an important monastic establishment and with its buildings and grounds occupied nearly a quarter of the space within the walls. There were the hot springs which were administered by the Prior until the dissolution. The city was famous for its woollen cloth, as is evidenced by Chaucer's Wife of Bath:

> *Of clooth-making she hadde swiche an haunt,*
> *She passed hem of Ypres and of Gaunt,*

and Leland wrote in 1542 that 'the town hath of a long time since been continually most maintained by making of cloth', though he added that recently 'it hath somewhat decayed', and eighty years later the Mayor was writing 'we are a very poor little city, our clothmen much decayed, and many of their workmen relieved by the city'.

Bath was still a small, medieval-looking city as late as 1723, as is shown in William Stukeley's drawing and plan of that year, and indeed comparison with a map of 1572 shows how remarkably little change had taken place in the intervening hundred and fifty years. The walls still stood in their entirety. The spaces between the houses had been filled in and there had been some demolition and rebuilding, but hardly any expansion. The Georgian boom had not yet got under way; only the brand-new Trim Street (begun 1707), just outside the north wall was its herald.

In the next hundred years Bath exploded from little more than a large village to one of the most important towns in England, a centre of fashion and a showpiece of town architecture. The initiation of this transformation is credited to three men: Richard Nash, John Wood and Ralph Allen. Richard 'Beau' Nash was the first to arrive, coming to Bath in 1705 at the age of thirty-one as a professional gambler after a somewhat erratic career. He suddenly found his metier when the Master of Ceremonies, one Captain Webster, was killed in a duel and he was offered the succession. Bath already had, of course, a national reputation for its medicinal hot waters—eminent patients had included Charles II's Queen, Catherine of Braganza, in 1663, James II's Queen, Mary of Modena, in 1687, and Queen Anne in 1692, 1702 and 1703—but it was a badly governed town of violence and scandal, and there was no incentive for the genteel visitor to prolong his or her stay. Nash was to change all that. By sheer force of personality, he imposed a code of manners and instituted a regime which enabled Bath to become the second capital of English society, winning universal acknowledgment for his title of King of Bath. Nash remained active into his eighties and did not die until 1761. Although by then his influence was not quite so powerful and Bath was perhaps not quite so uniquely fashionable, the expansion of the city continued unabated until the end of the century and beyond.

Ralph Allen came to Bath in 1710 as a seventeen-year-old assistant to the postmistress, taking over as postmaster two years later. He was an able man of business and made a large fortune by securing the contract for the cross-posts and reorganizing them. In applying his talents to the development of the Combe Down quarries, which he also controlled, Allen made a significant contribution to the expansion of the city by reducing the cost of its basic material. And Prior Park, the house which John Wood built for him, although essentially a country mansion is also very much a part of Bath and ranks as its largest and finest single domestic building. But it is of course Wood, the last of the three to arrive in the city, who is architecturally by far the most important. Although a Bathonian his early career was in Yorkshire and London. He returned to his native city in 1727 as it seemed to him to be on the verge of expansion. Although as we have seen the shape and size of the city were still medieval, some building was in progress and pre-Wood houses of the early eighteenth century are still to be found in Trim Street (mentioned above), Westgate Street, Abbey Churchyard, Green Street, Broad Street (see the Saracen's Head, page 121) and elsewhere. A new Pump Room had been built as early as 1704–6, i.e. before Nash's arrival. Killigrew and Greenway were competent craftsmen-architects at work during this period. A little later, and exactly contemporary with Wood, the Bristol architect John Strahan started laying out new streets to the west of the city. Nevertheless, considering that Nash had already been in office for twenty years and his reign was reaching its peak, there must have been an acute shortage of accommodation for the crowds of fashionable and wealthy visitors, and what there was would have seemed old-fashioned and provincial. So Wood timed his return just right and caught a boom which was going to happen anyway. He took magnificent advantage of his opportunity. Both as a designer and as an entrepreneur he was well ahead of any local rivals. His London experience had made him up-to-date in the fashionable Palladian idiom, and he evidently had a natural flair for business and for public relations. His first work in Bath was for a landowner-developer, the Duke of Chandos, for whom he built a court of houses on a site which the duke had bought from St. John's Hospital. But after some negotiations with another landowner, Dr. Gay, had proved abortive, Wood decided to act as his own principal. His technique, which was imitated by numerous successors, was to obtain an area of land on long lease or freehold; draw up a design for the façade of a terrace of houses; and sublease the individual plots to builders who were free to plan their interior layouts as they wished so long as they adhered to Wood's design for the exterior. It was a system which worked perfectly so long as the demand for accommodation kept up, as the builders could let or sell their houses before they were built and on the strength of these agreements obtain loans from their

QUEEN SQUARE, north side

bankers. It was not until later in the century that demand became less insistent and more selective, which sometimes meant financial disaster for the architect-developer.

John Wood the elder is conspicuously the most famous of Bath architects and perhaps of all English provincial architects. How far is this rating justified? A balanced assessment is not easy. In his day he suffered from little local competition and he enjoyed a busy career, but he died in 1754 at the age of forty-nine and much the greater part of Georgian Bath was built after his death. As a town-planner his great reputation derives on the one hand from his own description of the 'Designs' which he prepared at the age of twenty-one (see page 142), and on the other from the magnificent sequence Queen Square/Circus/Crescent for which he was partially responsible. But the grandiose and fanciful 'Designs' were highly impractical and apart from the inclusion of a Circus do not have much relation to what actually went up. And the evidence shows that what is often called 'Wood's Bath' developed stage by stage over forty years with innovations and modifications as the work progressed. Baldwin's Bathwick New Town, though incomplete, is a better example of adherence to a preconceived plan. Nevertheless Wood was the pioneer who brought Bath from being an insignificant little town into the mainstream of European architecture, and at his best, with such works as the Circus, Prior Park and the Bristol Exchange, he can stand comparison with any of his English contemporaries.

On Wood's death his son, also John, succeeded to his practice at the age of twenty-seven. He had already been working as his father's assistant on the Liverpool Exchange and elsewhere. The elder Wood was the purest of Palladians—it would have been unthinkable to work in any other style at the time, and anyway he was an enthusiastic antiquarian and admirer of Rome—and his son continued basically in the same idiom. Bath architecture was still a Wood monopoly, and the younger man's contribution was at least as extensive as his father's. He completed the grand sequence of 'Wood's Bath' by building the Circus, barely started when his father died, and adding Brock Street and the Crescent; while to the east of the Circus he built the new Assembly Rooms and the surrounding streets. It was not until the 1770s that a new generation of architects appeared. Palmer, Baldwin and Eveleigh dominated the scene for the last quarter of the eighteenth century, during which more of Georgian Bath was built than in any comparable period. Palmer was the first to appear but Baldwin was the most talented. Although he was aggressive and unreliable and had a chequered career—he was sacked by the city and later went bankrupt—he did a great deal of work, much of it of high quality, and Baldwin must be ranked next to the Woods among Bath architects. As was to be expected he and his contemporaries broke away from Palladianism ,old-fashioned by the mid-seventies, to follow the lighter, more shallow but more elegant style associated with Robert Adam and James Wyatt—Adam himself designed Pulteney Bridge which leads into Baldwin's new Bathwick, and prepared interesting unexecuted plans for this estate.

It is not too much of an over-simplification to date Bath's golden age of architecture from Wood's return to Bath in 1727; ascribe it a length of a hundred years; and divide it into four roughly equal phases. The first twenty-seven years to his death in 1754 can be called Wood I; Wood II follows for over twenty years. The third period can be called Palmer-Baldwin-Eveleigh and runs from Baldwin's Guildhall of 1776 until the turn of the century.

The final phase coincides with the first quarter of the new century and can be associated with the name of Pinch. Although there were other architects, John Pinch the elder dominated his profession during this period. He is an under-rated architect whose contribution to Bath's domestic buildings is considerable and of high quality. He also designed St. Mary, Bathwick, the prettiest of Bath's many Gothic revival churches. Of this period there are three interesting neo-Classical buildings by London architects, namely Doric House (J. M. Gandy), the Free-masons' Hall, now the Friends Meeting House (William Wilkins) and Partis College (S. and P. F. Page). Also dating from the early nineteenth century are a number of attractive villas up Bathwick Hill and elsewhere. The Bath architect H. E. Goodridge, whose career ran from 1819 to the 1850s, progressed from neo-Grecian through Gothic to Victorian Romanesque; he built a tower on Lansdown for William Beckford to a remarkable design, perhaps inspired by his eccentric client. With the slightly later G. P. Manners who restored the Abbey and built St. Michael's and the Bluecoat School, we come well into the Victorian era.

Victorian architecture is now much more indulgently regarded than it was even twenty years ago. All the same, and in spite of a number of attractive buildings, it is permissible to be thankful that Bath, though remaining a popular spa, was out of the mainstream of national expansion and did not undergo much change at the town's centre—the outskirts were a different matter. The most prolific and the best of the Bath Victorian architects were James Wilson and his partner W. J. Willcox. Between them they covered a considerable variety of styles: neo-Classical at the Moravian Chapel, pre-Pugin Gothic at St. Stephen, Lansdown, Tudor at Kingswood School, other kinds of Gothic at the Royal School, St. Paul's and two Baptist chapels, mid-Victorian office-block Classical for the banks at the top of Milsom Street, a French roof for the Grand Pump Room Hotel, and Italianate for the remarkable Walcot Schools in Guinea Lane. Their work is always worth looking at. By other architects there are the two stations early in the reign, and at its end the startling Empire Hotel by Davis and the handsome extensions to the Guildhall and Pump Room by Brydon.

Contrary to what is sometimes believed, the Bath Victorians admired their Georgian heritage—a guide book of 1876 calls the Circus 'magnificent', the Crescent 'splendid', the Guildhall 'noble' and the Assembly Rooms 'simply perfect'—and they destroyed very little. Unfortunately they permitted themselves a good deal of superficial 'improvements' which are hard to excuse. Apart from the festoons of drain pipes, the insertion of plate-glass shop-fronts and the alteration or removal of parapets, there was a wholesale mutilation of house windows which spoils the proportions of the elevations to an extent which is not always fully realized. This was so widespread that one sometimes has to refer to old prints to appreciate the original fenestration. The removal of glazing bars is obvious, and easily remedied; not so the cutting-down of windows at the base—every single house in the Circus and the Crescent suffered this—the splaying back and painting of reveals, and the insertion of iron balconies. The wooden blind-hoods might at least be removed now that the blinds have nearly all long since ceased to function. This sort of thing, though now taking different forms, has not entirely ceased. The North and South Parades are perhaps the worst example of many, though even in the Crescent the yellow door and blinds at No. 22 demonstrate how idiosyncracy can spill over into bad manners.

BLUECOAT SCHOOL, Sawclose

Space has dictated a limitation to the Gazetteer in this book and it seemed sensible to impose a terminal date. Nothing therefore is included after the First World War. Assessment of recent architecture is never easy, and it would be an unfair, if tempting, generalization to say that this omission excludes little that is noteworthy though a great deal that is conspicuous. The better buildings tend to be away from the centre; examples are the Catholic Church of St. Alphege in Oldfield Park by Sir Giles Gilbert Scott (1929) and, in the 1960s, Leonard Manasseh's Rotork factory on the river bank and another Catholic Church, Martin Fisher's SS. Peter and Paul on Combe Down. Building between the wars in central Bath was usually in a cautious neo-Georgian intended to blend in with the rest of the city. The new Post Office, the Forum Cinema and several shop blocks are examples. Work since 1945 has been more extensive, and bolder. Initially there were considerable bomb-damaged areas which would have had to be cleared and rebuilt in any event. This has been followed by further demolition, which has included some eighteenth-century housing which was stated to be substandard, noticeably in the Ballance Street area west of Lansdown Road. There are a great many eighteenth and early nineteenth-century rows of small artisan houses dotted around Bath. These are not of themselves of any great architectural merit and have often become delapidated, but they have considerable charm and are an essential part of the Bath scene. It has been suggested that the possibilities of renovating and modernizing these terraces have not always been fully explored, and their replacement by butter-coloured slabs of offices and flats is to be regretted. Stylistically, neo-Georgian is now out of fashion and is confined to particularly sensitive areas, such as the block which replaced the Grand Pump Room Hotel and the new extension to the Pump Room itself. Modern buildings, the architects feel, ought to look modern. While this view deserves respect it cannot be said that any recent building in central Bath has evoked much enthusiasm, and some of it, such as the 'Harvey block' opposite the Guildhall, has been strongly criticized. The problem of appropriate fenestration in a local context and a modern idiom seems to defeat everyone. Features which are not universally admired are the over-frequent mansard roofs, black and conspicuous, and the insistence on Bath stone, usually artificial for reasons of cost. This latter rule, well-meaningly introduced between the wars when planning restrictions were in their infancy, is an inappropriate handicap on modern designers and should be reconsidered. In the post-war period it would have been much more to the point to limit the height of buildings; there is no need for nine-storey blocks in a small town like Bath.

This introduction to Bath's architecture can end on a happier note by mentioning something which will attract no criticism, namely the scheme for cleaning and restoring the fronts of Bath's Georgian houses which has been in operation during recent years. One has only to look at the photographs in Mr. Ison's book, published in 1948, to appreciate the transformation that has taken place since then. Of course there is still plenty to do, but the progress which has been made is remarkable. The cost of the work is split between the Historic Buildings Council, the local authority and the houseowner, who deserve the gratitude of resident and visitor alike.

C

A Chronology of Bath Buildings, 1700–1900

1702–14	ANNE
1705	*Richard 'Beau' Nash (born 1674) arrives in Bath*
1706	Orange Grove (reconstructed 1897)
1707	Trim Street started (General Wolfe's House built *c.* 1720)
c. 1707–*c.* 1727	*Thomas Greenway, mason and architect, working in Bath*
1710	*Ralph Allen (born 1693) arrives in Bath*
1713	Saracen's Head, Broad Street
1714–27	GEORGE I
1719–22	*William Killigrew, joiner and architect, working in Bath*
c. 1720	General Wade's House, Abbey Churchyard
1727–60	GEORGE II
1727	Widcombe Manor House
1726–40	*John Strahan, architect, working in Bath*
1727–54	*John Wood the elder, architect, working in Bath*
1727	Ralph Allen's Town House, Lilliput Alley (John Wood the elder)
c. 1727	Beaufort Square (John Strahan)
1728–36	Queen Square (John Wood the elder)
c. 1730	Beau Nash's House, St. John's Court, Sawclose (Thomas Greenway)
1734	Orange Grove Obelisk (John Wood the elder)
1735–50	Prior Park (John Wood the elder, completed by Richard Jones)
1736	Rosewell House, Kingsmead Square (attributed to John Strahan)
1738	Queen Square Obelisk (John Wood the elder)
1738–42	Royal Mineral Water Hospital, Upper Borough Walls (John Wood the elder) (extensions 1850–60)
1740	No. 41 Gay Street (John Wood the elder)
1740–43	North and South Parades (John Wood the elder)
1742	Linley House, No. 1 Pierrepont Place (John Wood the elder)
c. 1745–*c.* 1777	*Thomas Jelly, builder and architect, working in Bath*
c. 1750	No. 1, Terrace Walk
1752	King Edward's School, Broad Street (Thomas Jelly)
1754	The Circus (John Wood the elder)
1754–*c.* 1780	*John Wood the younger, architect, working in Bath*
1755–75	*Thomas Warr Atwood, City Architect, working in Bath*

1760–1820	GEORGE III
1761	*Death of Beau Nash*
1762	Sham Castle (Richard Jones)
1764	*Death of Ralph Allen*
1765	Countess of Huntingdon's Chapel, Vineyards
1765–67	Octagon Chapel, Milsom Street (Thomas Lightoler)
1767–68	Brock Street (John Wood the younger)
1767–75	Royal Crescent (John Wood the younger)
1768–1805	*John Palmer, City Architect, working in Bath*
1768	The Paragon (Thomas Warr Atwood)
1768	St. James's Parade (Thomas Jelly and John Palmer)
1768–71	'New' Assembly Rooms (John Wood the younger)
1769–74	Pulteney Bridge (Robert Adam)
c. 1772	Alfred Street (John Wood the younger)
1772–73	'New' Prison, Grove Street (Thomas Warr Atwood)
1775–78	The Hot Bath (John Wood the younger)
1775–95	*Thomas Baldwin, City Architect, working in Bath*
1776	The Guildhall (Thomas Baldwin) (additions 1891)
1777–90	St. Swithin, Walcot (Thomas Jelly and John Palmer)
1778	Northumberland Buildings, Wood Street (Thomas Baldwin)
1782	Somersetshire Buildings, Milsom Street (Thomas Baldwin)
1785–93	*John Eveleigh, architect, working in Bath*
1786–95	The Pump Room (Thomas Baldwin and John Palmer) (extensions 1897)
1786–1813	*Charles Harcourt Masters, surveyor and architect, working in Bath*
1788	Camden Crescent (John Eveleigh)
1788	Laura Place and Great Pulteney Street (Thomas Baldwin)
1789–93	Lansdown Crescent (John Palmer)
1790–94	St. James's Square (John Palmer)
1790–1820	Somerset Place (John Eveleigh)
1791–c. 1801	Grosvenor Hotel, now Grosvenor Place (John Eveleigh)
c. 1790	The Cross Bath (Thomas Baldwin)
1791	Bath Street (Thomas Baldwin)
1795	Kensington Chapel, London Road (John Palmer)
1796	Sydney Hotel, now Holburne of Menstrie Museum (Charles Harcourt Masters) (reconstructed 1913–16)
1796–1810	Kennet and Avon Canal
1798–1810	Norfolk Crescent
1804–5	The Theatre Royal (George Dance the younger and John Palmer)
c. 1805	Doric House, Sion Hill (Joseph Michael Gandy)

c. 1805	Widcombe Crescent and Terrace (Charles Harcourt Masters)
1808–27	*John Pinch the elder, architect, working in Bath*
1808	'New' Sydney Place (John Pinch the elder)
1814–20	St. Mary, Bathwick (John Pinch the elder) (chancel 1873–75)
1814–49	*John Pinch the younger, architect, working in Bath*
1815–16	Walcot Methodist Chapel (William Jenkins)
1817–19	Freemasons' Hall, now Friends Meeting House, York Street (William Wilkins)
1817–30	Cavendish Crescent (John Pinch the elder)
1819–63	*Henry Edmund Goodridge, architect, working in Bath*

1820–30	GEORGE IV
c. 1820	St. Mary's Buildings, Wells Road
1820–60	*George Philip Manners, City Architect, working in Bath*
1823–27	Beckford's Tower, Lansdown (Henry Edmund Goodridge)
1824	'The Bazaar', Quiet Street
1825–27	Partis College (Samuel and Philip Flood Page)
1827	Cleveland Bridge (Henry Edmund Goodridge)
1827–44	*Edward Davis, City Architect, working in Bath*
1829–32	St. Saviour, Larkhall (John Pinch the elder or younger) (chancel 1882)

1830–37	WILLIAM IV
1835–37	St. Michael, Broad Street (George Philip Manners)
1837	Victoria Park Obelisk (George Philip Manners)

1837–1901	VICTORIA
1840	Great Western Railway (Isambard Kingdom Brunel)
1840–85	*James Wilson, architect, working in Bath*
1840–45	St. Stephen, Lansdown Road (James Wilson) (chancel 1882)
1841	Bath Savings Bank, now Register Office, Charlotte Street (George Alexander)
c. 1844	Royal and Argyll Hotels, Manvers and Dorchester Streets
1844–82	St. Paul, Prior Park (Joseph John Scoles)
1845	The Dispensary, Cleveland Place (Henry Edmund Goodridge)
1845	Moravian Chapel, now Christian Science Church, Charlotte Street (James Wilson)
1854	Percy Chapel, now Elim Chapel, Charlotte Street (H. E. and A. S. Goodridge)
1856–58	The Royal School, Lansdown Road (James Wilson)

1857–1904	*Charles Edward Davis, City Architect, working in Bath*
1860	The Bluecoat School, Sawclose (Manners and Gill)
1861–67	St. John's Catholic Church, South Parade (Charles Hansom)
1865–c. 1910	*William John Willcox, architect, working in Bath*
1865	National Westminster Bank, Milsom Street and George Street (William John Willcox)
1869–70	Green Park Station
1872	Manvers Street Baptist Chapel (Wilson and Willcox)
1872–74	St. Paul, now Holy Trinity, Monmouth Street (Wilson, Willcox and Wilson)
1873–75	St. Mary Bathwick, chancel (George Edmund Street)
1882	St. Saviour Larkhall, chancel (Charles Edward Davis)
1882	St. Stephen Lansdown, chancel (William John Willcox)
1891–97	Extensions to Guildhall and Pump Room (John McKean Brydon)
1899–1901	Empire Hotel (Charles Edward Davis)

Key to Numbers on Plans

(References beginning with A to D are in Plan 1, those beginning with E to H in Plan 2)

- 1. The Abbey   GY
- 2. Abbey Green   GZ
- 3. Alfred Street   FV
- 4. Assembly Rooms   FV
- 5. Bath Street   FZ
- 6. 'The Bazaar'   FX
- 7. Beau Nash's House   FY
- 8. Beaufort Square   FY
- 9. Beckford's Tower   BQ
- 10. Bluecoat School   FY
- 11. Brock Street   EV
- 12. Camden Crescent   CR
- 13. Cavendish Crescent   BR
- 14. Cemetery Chapel, Walcot   CS
- 15. Christian Science Church   EX
- 16. The Circus   EV
- 17. Cleveland Bridge   CS
- 18. Countess of Huntingdon's Chapel   GV
- 19. Cross Bath   FZ
- 20. The Dispensary   CR
- 21. Doric House   BR
- 22. Elim Chapel   EX
- 23. Empire Hotel   HY
- 24. Friends Meeting House   GZ
- 25. No. 41 Gay Street   FW
- 26. Great Pulteney Street   CS
- 27. Great Western Railway   CT
- 28. Green Park Station   EY
- 29. Grosvenor Place   DR
- 30. Guildhall   GY
- 31. Holburne of Menstrie Museum   DS
- 32. Holy Trinity   EX
- 33. Hot Bath   FZ
- 34. Kennet and Avon Canal   DT
- 35. Kensington Chapel   DR
- 36. King Edward's School   GW
- 37. Lansdown Crescent   CR
- 38. Laura Place   HX
- 39. Linley House   HZ
- 40. Lodge Style   DU
- 41. Manvers Street Baptist Chapel   CT
- 42. National Westminster Bank   FW
- 43. Norfolk Crescent   BS
- 44. North and South Parades   HZ
- 45. Northumberland Buildings   FX
- 46. Obelisks
    - (a) Orange Grove   HY
    - (b) Queen Square   FX
    - (c) Victoria Park   BS
- 47. The Octagon Chapel   GX
- 48. Orange Grove   HY
- 49. The Paragon   GV
- 50. Partis College   AR
- 51. 'Pinch's Folly'   CS
- 52. Prior Park   DU
- 53. Prison   HW
- 54. Pulteney Bridge   HX
- 55. Pump Room   GY
- 56. Queen Square   FX
- 57. Ralph Allen's Town House   HZ
- 58. Rebecca Fountain   GY
- 59. Register Office   EX
- 60. Roman Baths   GZ
- 61. Rosewell House   FY
- 62. Royal and Argyll Hotels   CT
- 63. Royal Crescent   BS
- 64. Royal Mineral Water Hospital   GX
- 65. The Royal School   CR
- 66. St. James's Parade   CT
- 67. St. James's Square   CS
- 68. St. John's Catholic Church   HZ
- 69. St. Mary   DS
- 70. St. Mary's Buildings   CT
- 71. St. Michael   GX
- 72. St. Paul   DU
- 73. St. Saviour   DR
- 74. St. Stephen   CR
- 75. St. Swithin   CS
- 76. Saracen's Head   GX
- 77. Sham Castle   DS

78. Somerset Place   BR
79. Somersetshire Buildings   FX
80. Sydney Place   DS
81. Terrace Walk   HZ
82. Theatre Royal   FY
83. General Wade's House   GY

84. Walcot Methodist Chapel   CR
85. Walcot Street   GW
86. Widcombe Crescent and Terrace   DT
87. Widcombe Manor House   DT
88. General Wolfe's House   FX

PLAN 1: Bath

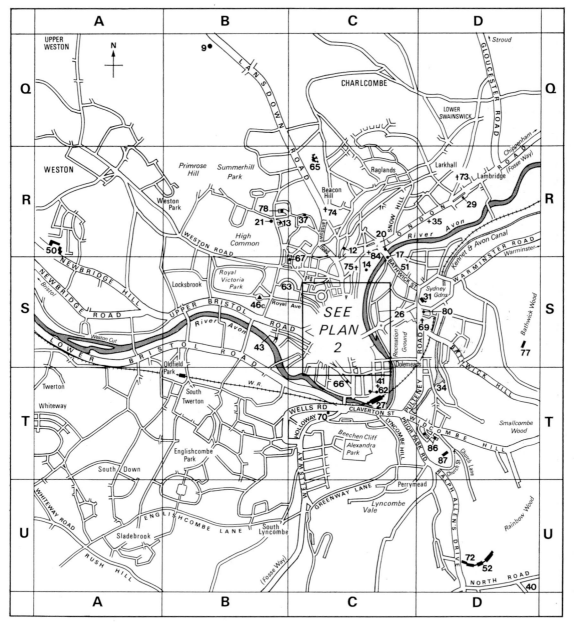

PLAN 2

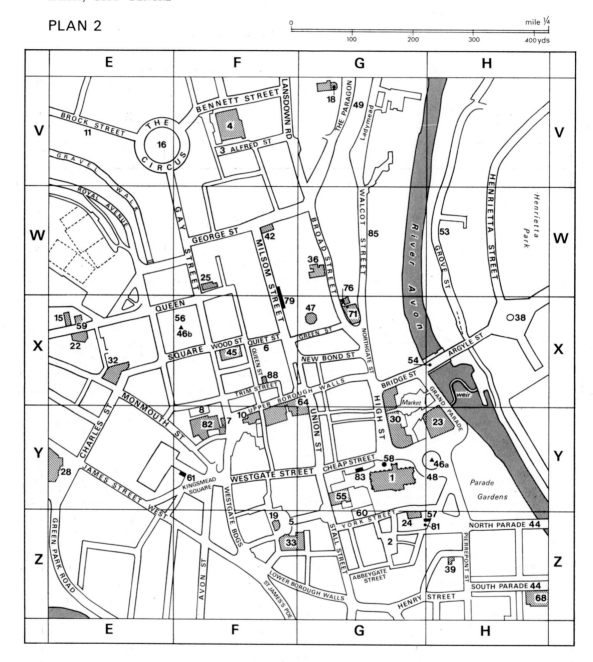

THIS list includes all the important buildings which every visitor to Bath should see if he can. These are marked ●. Otherwise, the selection pretends to no significance other than the personal taste of the compiler, though the buildings chosen are mostly either conspicuous (e.g. the Station, the Empire Hotel) or worth seeking out (e.g. Partis College, Widcombe Crescent). A reasonable range of Victoriana has been attempted; there is nothing after 1914. Omission carries no implication whatever other than shortage of space.

BATH ABBEY, the west front

●THE ABBEY [Plan 2 GY1]

The bishop of the Somerset diocese is called the Bishop of Bath and Wells, and the Abbey looks like a cathedral, albeit a small one. So any visitor could reasonably conclude that the bishop has two sees. This is not so however. Wells is the true cathedral city, with Dean, Chapter, Close and Bishop's Palace; Bath has only the empty title, and the Abbey has for long been simply the main parish church of Bath. The history of this anomaly goes back to 1088, when the then Bishop of Wells, one John de Villula, also known as John of Tours, physician and chaplain to William Rufus, moved his see from Wells to Bath. This was in accordance with Norman church policy, promulgated at the Council of London in 1075, that sees ought to be in larger rather than smaller towns. At the same time he changed his title to Bishop of Bath. Considerable dissension ensued, not surprisingly, between the canons of Wells and the monks of Bath, especially about the election of bishops. The bishops eventually returned to Wells, and the double title was confirmed by Pope Innocent IV in 1245. But Bishop King signed himself 'Oliver Bathe' in 1499, and Leland referred to him as 'Bishop of Bath' in 1542.

The church itself also misleads in that its uniform appearance conceals a long and complicated building history. As John Britton wrote in 1824, 'Bath Abbey Church is mostly of a Protestant age, although its design is monastic.' In other words, much of what we see today is the result of a series of attempts by later generations to recreate what they believed the early Tudor builders would have put up if they had had the time and the money to

BATH ABBEY from the north-east

finish what they had started. Looked at in this light, the Abbey is undoubtedly a successful piece of pastiche. Only in an occasional detail (the pinnacles and polygonal turrets, and perhaps the nave flying buttresses) did the nineteenth-century restorers try to improve on the original design.

There were two earlier buildings before the present church. All we know about the Saxon abbey is that in 957 it was referred to as being of 'wonderful workmanship', and that in it, in 973, Edgar was crowned first King of all England. Even its site is uncertain. At the end of the eleventh century John de Villula, very probably to mark Bath's new status as his see, started to build. His church was very large, much longer than the present building, the whole of which is built on the foundations of its nave. Nothing definite is known about its appearance; it can be surmised that its ground plan resembled that of Gloucester and Professor Boase considers that the west front may

BATH ABBEY,
the west door,
1617

have been like Tewkesbury. French parallels suggest themselves, especially in view of Bishop John's origins. Some fragments survive; these are mainly below the present floor level, but at the east end of the present church, i.e. at the position of the crossing of the Norman abbey, can be seen on the exterior two groups of column bases, and inside about three-quarters of an arch which originally led from the south aisle of the nave into the south transept. The part of this arch above the capital looks as though it had been rebuilt and heightened at some time during the twelfth century, possibly after a fire which occurred in 1137. Outside the

church the block of houses known as Orange Grove (q.v.) may be built partly on the foundations of the Norman south chancel aisle. Some Norman stonework is also preserved (now in the choir vestry) including two capitals of high quality. Piecing together these clues is an interesting task awaiting a future student.

Oliver King, who was principal secretary to Henry VII after having held the same office under Henry VI, Edward IV and Edward V, was appointed Bishop in 1495. By that time the monastic community had become reduced in size and the old church was much too large. Moreover, it was

in a ruinous condition. So in 1499 or 1500 King
began to build his new church. He was inspired,
Sir John Harington says, by a dream in which he
saw the Holy Trinity, with angels climbing up and
down a ladder to heaven, at the foot of which was
an olive tree supporting a crown, and heard a
voice say 'let an Olive establish the Crown and
let a King restore the Church'. He took the first
part of this message to refer to his christian name
and his support for the Tudor monarchy, and the
ladder and the angels, the olive tree and the crown
are to be seen (much restored) on his west front.
The fact that William Birde was appointed Prior
at this time may also have had some significance,
for Birde proved an enthusiastic collaborator in
the building programme. (As a monastic establishment Bath was administered by a prior under the
bishop as abbot; strictly speaking it should be
called a Priory.)

The starting date of 1499 makes Oliver King's
Abbey very late among major English pre-
dissolution churches, but on the other hand as an
example of fan-vaulting on a large scale it was
comparatively early, and the masons employed by
the Bishop promised him that there should 'be
none so goodly neither in England nor in France'.
These masons were Robert and William Vertue,
who also worked for the King; they built Henry
VII's chapel at Westminster Abbey (1500–12) and
William, after Robert's death, built St. George's
Chapel, Windsor (c. 1507–28). It seems likely that
the church was always intended to be fan-vaulted
in all parts, although the nave vault was not in
fact installed until 1869.

'The church', says Pevsner, 'is throughout quite
exceptionally uniform in design.' This uniformity
was largely dictated by the decision to use the
foundations of the Norman nave. The old nave
had nine bays; three were allotted to the chancel,
one to the tower and transepts, and five to the new
nave. This accounts for the close, and unusual,
similarity between the chancel and nave, and for
the strange flattened rectangle shape of the tower
and the narrowness of the transepts. Externally one
notices the relatively low aisles, the tall clerestory
windows, the even taller, slender windows in the
transepts, the square-headed east window, and the
steeply sloping flying buttresses. The west front
has already been mentioned. In addition to the

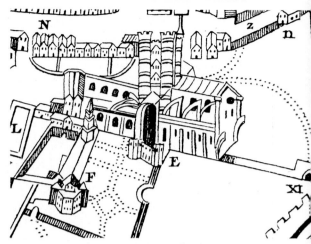

BATH ABBEY about 1572

sculpture illustrating Oliver King's dream, the
original scheme included the two figures on each
side of the doorway, the figures on each side of
the ladders and the now much-worn angels above
the window. The central statues of Christ en-
throned and Henry VII are replacements by Sir
George Frampton. Inside the most striking architectural feature is the impressive fan vaulting
throughout the church; especially beautiful are the
smaller aisle vaults with pendants like those which
the Vertues included a little later in the Henry VII
Chapel at Westminster. The effect of the large
windows, mercifully not all filled with stained
glass, is very fine.

Now for the building history. What we should
most like to know is what the church looked like
at the dissolution. But the evidence is scanty. Taking the east end first, it is usually assumed that the
present chancel vault is original and was completed before 1518. This is because it includes the
arms of Cardinal Adrian di Costello, King's successor as bishop, who was a dubious character and
a permanent absentee living in Rome. He was
deprived of his bishopric in that year, and it is
presumed that his arms would not have been put
up in the vault after his dismissal. However it is
obvious that the vault and the square-headed east
window do not fit together and cannot have been
part of the same scheme. If the window is original,
the conclusion can only be, as Dr. Peter Kidson
puts it, that the choir was 'designed to receive
a very shallow vault, perhaps based on a four-

centred section, like that of St. George's Chapel Windsor'. An alternative, and perhaps more likely, assumption is that the east window took its present shape at some later date.

As to the rest of the church, Leland, writing about 1542, says that 'Oliver King, Bishop of Bath, began of late days a right goodly new church at the west part of the old church of St. Peter and finished a great part of it. The residue was since made by the Priors of Bath.' In spite of this strong contemporary evidence, there is considerable doubt as to whether the church was really finished before the dissolution and in particular whether the western part was vaulted. In any event, not only did any building which may have been in progress come to an abrupt halt in 1535, but a few years later glass, iron, bells and a large quantity of lead were sold off to 'certain Merchants'. Some of these materials may have been stacked on site

ready for installation, but others were stripped from the fabric. This naturally led to rapid deterioration, and makes it difficult to say whether the work done by the Elizabethans, of which we have some records, was restoration or new building. In 1560 or 1572 (the authorities differ) the Abbey and its churchyard, which had been sold into private hands at the dissolution, were given to the city. The church was then described as 'uncovered and much ruined, as it had long stood after the dissolution, yet the walls of the great tower and of most part of the church were then standing'. This description is confirmed by the *View of the City of Bath in the Year 1572* which was reproduced in John Wood's *Essay*. The provenance of this plan has been queried but the date must be broadly correct. The drawing of the Abbey is crude but it shows clearly the remains of two Norman arches at the east end; the unfinished south transept; the unroofed nave; and, perhaps most interestingly, no large window at the east end but instead two small lancets with a round window above—the interpretation of these is difficult.

It was at about this time that work began again. In or before 1572 Peter Chapman, a distinguished soldier, put a stone and wood roof and a new parapet on the north chancel aisle, which became known as 'Chapman's aisle' (they were removed by Manners in 1833). In 1574 Elizabeth I visited Bath and as a result granted letters patent authorising collections in every part of the kingdom for seven years for the completion of the church. Some of the money was misappropriated, but in spite of this a timber roof covered with blue slate was put over the 'upper part' (presumably the chancel) and the north transept. At this period the chancel was 'inclosed, and fitted up for divine service' by Thomas Bellot, steward to the great Lord Burghley, who also 'raised the south part of the cross aisle' (i.e. the south transept) 'near from the ground' and 'lofted and leaded' the tower.

Things began to move faster on the arrival as bishop of James Montague in 1608. Urged on by his distant relative Sir John Harington of Kelston, who had been grumbling about the state of the Abbey for many years past, Bishop Montague set to with such vigour that all the work was completed by the time of his translation to Winchester

BATH ABBEY, vault of south chancel aisle

BATH ABBEY, interior towards east

in 1616, including a wood and plaster roof to the nave and its aisles, which had been entirely open on his arrival. One of the additions at this period was the fine west door, which was given by the bishop's brother, Sir Henry Montague, Lord Chief Justice of the King's Bench. A small clergy vestry was added in the corner between the south transept and the chancel; the ceiling of this is of interest as it shows what Bishop Montague's nave roof looked like before it was replaced by fan vaulting in 1869.

A print by J. C. Nattes shows the interior of the Abbey as it was in 1806. The nave was an open space and was not used for worship which was confined to the choir. Here there were two tiers of galleries in the aisles, box-pews, a big three-decker pulpit, and a fine organ under the tower surmounted by statues. All these were swept away during the next seventy years. There were two great nineteenth-century restorations: 1824–33 by G. P. Manners, City Architect of Bath, and 1864–74 by Sir Gilbert Scott. Scott has a bad reputation as an over-restorer, but in this case his predecessor was no less ruthless. In the fashion of his time, Manners made drastic alterations in order to replace the existing structure with what he considered the medieval mason must (or ought to) have meant to build. His most controversial additions were the pinnacles on the flying buttresses and turrets. After he had added these to the north transept there was some local criticism, which Manners crushed by calling in a Mr. Garbett, 'the eminent architect, of Winchester', who, 'after a personal examination of the building', stated (apparently without producing any evidence) 'his decided opinion that it was the original intention of the architect that pinnacles should have been erected; and that those already placed on the north transept were in strict uniformity with the edifice'. After this pronouncement further opposition was clearly unthinkable; 'the "pinnacle warfare" was concluded'; and 'it was directed that in addition to those on the choir, nave and transepts, the same ornaments should be placed on the four turrets of the main tower, as well as the eastern and western staircases'. (Scott later modified the pinnacles and the parapets.) Acting on the same principles Manners added the flying buttresses on the nave to match those on the chancel; and he moved the 'ponderous dial', i.e.

the clock, from the tower to the north transept 'on the well-founded apprehension that its weight might, in course of time, endanger the safety of the tower'. An improvement made at this time which no one would criticize was the final removal of the clutter of buildings which had accumulated against the north wall of the Abbey.

After Manners's, Scott's restorations seem relatively innocuous. He did a great deal of work, spread over ten years (1864–74). The initiative, and to a large extent the money, came from the energetic and well-to-do rector, Charles Kemble. Scott's best-known and most noticeable change was the replacement of the Jacobean timber roof of the nave by fan vaulting to match that of the chancel. This time there is not much doubt that the new work accords with what the original builders intended, and Scott's vault has been generally condoned. Certainly the Abbey would look very different if Scott had acted as a conscientious modern restorer would probably do and left Montague's roof in place. Scott and Kemble totally transformed the interior, removing the screen, galleries, box-pews and three-decker pulpit, moving the organ into the north transept, and installing the present pews. Gas lighting was introduced. A new reredos replaced the one carved by Samuel Tufnell of Westminster and given by General Wade in 1725, which was to Victorian eyes 'quite incongruous, designed in the Corinthian style, with pillars, architrave, frieze, and cornice, executed in marble'. There was of course a new pulpit, new altar rails, new tiles in the sanctuary, new reading desk, lectern and font. In fact neither trouble nor expense was spared to create the Victorian ideal of a medieval church interior.

Scott also restored Prior Birde's chantry chapel (begun 1515) in the south aisle of the chancel; it had previously been restored by E. Davis in 1833. But both restorations seem to have been discreet and no visitor should miss this beautiful little structure, with its own fan vault and Birde's arms surmounted by a mitre, his initials W.B. and his rebus (a bird) appearing in the decoration. Also to be noted is the handsome tomb of Bishop Montague in the north nave aisle. He died in 1618 as Bishop of Winchester, but asked to be buried in the church he had done so much to restore. It is by William Cure, mason and designer, and Nicholas Johnson, carver—the largest of the enormous number of monuments in the church. These are mostly on the walls and of the eighteenth and early nineteenth centuries. Note the (relatively plain) tablet to Beau Nash in the south aisle of the nave. Nearly all the stained glass is nineteenth century; there is some heraldic glass of about 1604–20 in the fourth window from the west in the north aisle. The wrought-iron screen in the north transept was originally the altar rail, probably by the Bristol smith William Edney, given by General Wade in 1725. Sold off at the 1833 restoration, it was bought by William Beckford and installed in his house in Lansdown Crescent. It was recovered for the Abbey in 1959. This fine work now suffers somewhat by being mounted in two tiers. The choir vestry on the south side of the nave was added by Sir Thomas Jackson in 1923; he had previously restored the west front. There has recently been yet another restoration and all the stonework has been cleaned.

ABBEY GREEN [Plan 2   GZ2]

A charming oasis right in the middle of the city, with its oval lawn, spreading plane tree and genial pub. Pevsner calls it 'a forlorn little square', an incredible adjective until one remembers how much cleaning-up has gone on in Bath since he wrote in 1958. These houses, of varying dates and no architectural eminence, group themselves together into a harmonious ensemble. Nos. 2 and 2A on the east side, once derelict and under threat of 'development', have been restored by the Bath Preservation Trust. The south-west corner has recently been bridged by an arch designed with exemplary tact for Marks and Spencer. This little enclave ought to be, and hopefully soon will be, entirely closed to motor traffic.

ALFRED STREET [Plan 2   FV3]
John Wood the younger c. 1772

One of the group of streets, including Bennett Street and Russel Street, aligned on the Assembly Rooms and laid out in the 1770s under the general plans and supervision of the younger Wood. The

ABBEY GREEN, east side

ABBEY GREEN, south side

individual houses were constructed by various different speculative builders, who were allowed some freedom over details, and it seems likely that it was one of these who was responsible for the doorway of No. 14, with its festoons, pendants, vases and central bust of King Alfred. This house also has a well-preserved wrought-iron lamp overthrow in front of the doorway.

ARGYLL HOTEL, see Royal and Argyll Hotels

• THE ASSEMBLY ROOMS [Plan 2 FV4]
John Wood the younger 1768–71
The 'New' or 'Upper' Assembly Rooms were first projected in 1765 as part of the expansion of the Upper Town and in competition with the 'Lower' Rooms in Terrace Walk south-east of the Abbey. The site originally chosen was at the north-west corner of Queen Square, where Queen's Parade now stands. These plans came to nothing, as did an ambitious scheme prepared by Robert Adam for the present site, the Committee deciding on grounds of cost to adopt the more modest designs of the younger Wood.

The positioning of the Assembly Rooms was a

ALFRED STREET, doorway of No. 14

D

missed opportunity. Although close to the Circus it does not relate to it, and the entrance looks on to the untidy backs of the Circus houses. Moving the site a few yards and turning it through an angle would have made the Rooms the 'fine building' with which the elder Wood intended to terminate the eastward vista from his Circus. The failure to do this is the more inexplicable in that Bennett Street and the other surrounding streets were apparently built later and aligned on the Assembly Rooms and not, as Pevsner says, the other way round.

The undistinguished site may possibly have affected the younger Wood's designing of the exterior. It is simple and rather dull, and certainly gives no hint of the splendid rooms inside. The south (Alfred Street) front is the best and also the least altered.

The interior consists of a corridor leading from the porticoed west entrance ('for chairs') to an octagonal antechamber, with the ballroom on the

ASSEMBLY ROOMS, the south front

ASSEMBLY ROOMS, ballroom

ASSEMBLY ROOMS, tearoom

left, the tearoom on the right, and the great octagon, originally the cardroom, in front. The room beyond the octagon to the east was added in 1777.

The Rooms, after years of neglect—in 1921 the ballroom was turned into a cinema and the tearoom into a saleroom and market—were bought by Mr. Ernest Cook in 1931 and presented to the National Trust. They were restored by the architect-historian Mowbray Green and reopened in 1938, only to be gutted by the Luftwaffe four years later. After some controversy as to whether they were worth preserving they were reconstructed in 1963 by Sir Albert Richardson; fortunately sufficient records survived to permit an accurate restoration. The 106 foot long ballroom is the largest eighteenth-century room in Bath (Guildhall 80 feet, Pump Room 60 feet); the five magnificent chandeliers were fortunately stored away and survived the bombing. The tearoom was the least damaged and is perhaps the most attractive of the interiors, with its two-tiered screen of columns, originally forming a musicians' gallery, at the west end.

The rooms are let by the National Trust to the City of Bath. On the reopening in 1963 the city, with the supine acquiescence of the Trust, introduced some ugly and inappropriate furnishings. The bar in the centre of the great octagon, in particular, would have been a disgrace to a motorway cafeteria. At the time of writing there is some hope of its removal.

BATH SAVINGS BANK, see Register Office

BATH STREET [Plan 2 FZ5]
Thomas Baldwin 1791
(see plate on p. 12)

'By far the most beautiful of Baldwin's street designs,' writes Ison; Pevsner calls it 'a perfect piece of design', and Bryan Little 'as good a piece of townscape as anything in England'. High,

but deserved, praise for this relatively short street
—the length overall, including the curved ends, is
only about 230 feet.

Bath Street was designed as a link between
bathing establishments; Baldwin aligned it on the
'New Private Baths' (now the King's Bath entrance to the Pump Room) which he had built in
1788, and he refaced the Cross Bath at the other
end to provide a balancing symmetrical termination. The street fans out into curved segments at
both ends to face the two baths, and the street and
the segments are lined on both sides with Ionic
colonnades. These colonnades had the practical
purpose of allowing the eighteenth-century visitor
to walk, or be carried, under cover from one bath
to another; they are, of course, the outstanding
feature of Bath Street, although the attractive
entablatures of the main first floor windows are
also worth looking at.

Bath Street is relatively well preserved; the
north front has recently been carefully rebuilt,
though it is perhaps a disappointment that the
shops on this side have been replaced with nothing
more interesting than the entrance to Corporation
offices.

'THE BAZAAR', Quiet Street [Plan 2   FX6]
Attributed to H. E. Goodridge 1824

Originally called 'The Auction Mart and
Bazaar', with a large domed room extending
through the first and second floors designed for
exhibitions, meetings and the like. It is an unusual
example for Bath of a Georgian building planned
from the first for a commercial purpose of this
type, and the elevation is clearly intended to impress. Ison, who is responsible for the attribution
to Goodridge, identifies the attic with its statue as
being modelled on the Choragic Monument of
Thrasyllus. The statues in the niches are by the
Irish sculptor Lucius Gahagan and represent
Commerce and Genius.

In the 1840s 'the Bazaar Room' was used for
services by a breakaway sect of Methodists calling
themselves 'Reformed Wesleyans'. For many
years the building has been an antique shop; its
well-preserved façade has recently been cleaned.

BEAU NASH'S HOUSE, Sawclose [Plan 2   FY7]
Thomas Greenway c. 1730

The celebrated Richard 'Beau' Nash, Master of

THE BAZAAR, Quiet Street

BEAU NASH'S HOUSE, Sawclose, the doorway

BEAUFORT SQUARE, east side

Ceremonies for over fifty years from 1705, was the man principally responsible for turning Bath into a centre of fashion. He is justly regarded as one of the three founders of the Georgian city, the others being John Wood the architect and Ralph Allen the entrepreneur. Nash lived successively in two of the houses in the block in the Sawclose known as St. John's Court, which was built by Greenway in the 1720s. The first of these, much altered internally, is now the 'Garrick's Head' public house. Wood describes it as 'the Palace of the King of Bath . . . the richest Sample of Building, till then executed, in the City'. Later Nash moved a few yards north to the house which has this handsome doorway.

The appearance of St. John's Court has been ruined by the addition in the last century of the present entrance to the Theatre Royal (q.v.). Beau Nash's doorway, which now faces abruptly on to the side wall of this entrance, originally had an open space in front from which it could be properly appreciated.

BEAUFORT SQUARE [Plan 2 FY8]
John Strahan c. 1727

Sometimes spelt Beauford; originally Beaufort Buildings, and named after the Duke of Beaufort.

Strahan was John Wood's greatest rival, and the latter's *Essay Towards a Description of Bath* is bitterly critical of his 'Piratical Architecture', but Wood is grudgingly forced to concede that these small houses 'have a Sort of Regularity to recom-

mend them'. In fact the design—which was of course originally quite uniform throughout—had a great deal of charm in its modest way, as can be seen from the restored frontage on the east side; many of the other houses are too mutilated to be recognizable. The continuous triglyph frieze is particularly attractive. The group gives the observer a vivid impression of the small-town atmosphere which characterized pre-Wood Bath.

The fourth side of Beaufort Square is taken up by the main front of the Theatre Royal (q.v.) of eighty years later. Although handsome, it rather overwhelms the unassuming little cottages which surround it.

BECKFORD'S TOWER, Lansdown [Plan 1 BQ9]
H. E. Goodridge 1823–27

In 1822 William Beckford, his finances reduced by extravagance and mismanagement, sold Fonthill and moved to Bath. The sale price of £330,000 and the residue of his West Indian fortune ensured

BECKFORD'S TOWER, Lansdown

that his penury was well gilded, and he bought for his retirement three adjoining houses in Lansdown Crescent (q.v.) and an extensive area of land reaching from behind the Crescent to the top of Lansdown Hill. Here, his passion for building unabated, he immediately embarked on the construction of a folly tower. His architect was a young local man, H. E. Goodridge, who prepared several designs, including one resembling a Gothic lighthouse. There is a contemporary reference to a 'Saxon' tower; whether this refers to the tower as built or to one of the discarded proposals is not clear.

The executed design may perhaps owe as much to Beckford as to Goodridge. It is certainly of great originality; 'crazy in the extreme' says Pevsner, who thinks it may have inspired the Glasgow architect 'Greek' Thomson, while Ison finds it reminiscent of Soane. The octagonal summit is at least identifiable as a version of the Choragic Monument of Lysicrates in Athens. The house at the base of the tower was richly decorated and furnished but Beckford never actually lived there.

After Beckford's death in 1844 his daughter, the Duchess of Hamilton, presented the tower and grounds to the Rector of Walcot for use as a cemetery. This action was probably inspired by Beckford's unfulfilled wish to be buried at the foot of his tower; this could not originally be carried out because the land was not consecrated. Beckford's sarcophagus was duly moved from the Abbey cemetery in 1848. Goodridge designed the rather heavily Romanesque gateway and wall to the new cemetery; in due course he also was buried inside.

In 1934, after a fire, the inside of the house was transformed into a mortuary chapel two storeys high with a tunnel vault. In 1971, by then badly decayed, the building was sold to Dr. and Mrs. Hilliard, since when the tower has been restored and opened to the public and the chapel converted back to a house—the first time, it would seem, that it has ever actually been lived in.

BLUECOAT SCHOOL, Sawclose [Plan 2 FY10]
Manners and Gill c. 1860 (see plate on p. 32)

Now used as municipal offices. It was originally known as the Charity School and was founded in 1711 by Robert Nelson and others for the free education of fifty boys and girls. John Wood the elder (born 1704) was one of its early pupils. Its original location is not known, but in 1722 a schoolhouse was built on the Sawclose site by William Killigrew. This was an interesting pre-Wood building but survives only in pictures, as it was demolished in 1859 and replaced by the present edifice, a striking specimen of mid-Victorian Jacobethan. Pevsner says of one of the Bath churches of just the same date that it demonstrates how intensely the Gothicists hated the Georgian of Bath. This building, considering it does not have the excuse of being a church, seems even more of a gesture of defiance, in spite of the concessions to Classicism in the clock turret and the porch. The architects have valiantly attempted to

BROCK STREET, No. 7

cram as wide an assortment of motifs as possible on to the limited site. The way the turret slices into the largest of the curly gables is perhaps what startles the spectator most in this remarkable elevation.

BROCK STREET [Plan 2 EV11]
John Wood the younger 1767–68

Brock Street is significant less for its own architectural merits than as the link between the Circus and the Royal Crescent, and thus a vital part of the Wood town plan as finally executed. The alignment is so arranged that the sweep of the Crescent suddenly bursts on the spectator as he emerges from Brock Street after walking from the Circus —a magnificent *coup de théâtre*, enhanced by the relatively modest scale and simple detailing of the Brock Street houses. The credit for this is due to the younger Wood, not the elder, for the latter's plan for the Circus was to keep the east and west subsidiary streets short and terminate each of them with a 'fine building' to close the vista. The change of plan was called for by the increased demand for houses in the 1760s, and the actual layout must have been, at least to some extent,

BROCK STREET, doorways of Nos. 15 and 16

conditioned by the slope of the ground. Nevertheless the effect was carefully contrived, as is shown by the exact alignment of the return fronts of the end houses of the Crescent with the western entrance to the Circus, Brock Street running straight between. A brilliant adaptation by the son of the father's plan.

As has been said, Wood deliberately kept the Brock Street elevations relatively plain. There has however been so much subsequent mutilation that the original appearance of the houses is almost impossible to visualize. An exception is No. 7, which was the least altered and has recently been beautifully restored. The doorways are particularly puzzling. Clearly there was originally some variation of treatment, but there have also been many later changes, such as the Italianate three-storied porches at Nos. 9 and 14. Is the Gothic doorway at No. 16 really part of the original scheme, as has been stated? Its style could be of the 1760s, but it surely would have been out of character for Wood to allow so striking a departure from conformity.

CAMDEN CRESCENT [Plan 1 CR12]
John Eveleigh 1788

Originally known as Upper Camden Place. Part of a large scheme which was to have consisted of a crescent of twenty-two houses, two flanking wings of five houses each, and a terrace to be called Lower Camden Place further down Lansdown Hill. Only the west wing and the western eighteen of the Crescent houses were finished; the reason for this was not the usual exhaustion of funds, but more dramatically 'a series of alarming landslips' which brought the work at the eastern end to a standstill. It was never resumed, and the Crescent remains truncated. The façade of the last house on the east, which naturally duplicated the pavilion treatment of the west end with its four three-quarter columns, had already been completed, and stood for many years as a picturesque Piranesi-like ruin.

Eveleigh's elevation—no one doubts Ison's attribution—is curiously old-fashioned for its date, echoing the north side of Queen Square of sixty years earlier. Its most noticeable feature, at any rate to architectural purists, is the odd number of columns (five) in the centre pavilion, resulting in the placing of one column under the middle of the pediment. This is often criticized as a solecism, but Eveleigh repeated the oddity at Grosvenor Place (q.v.) with variations—here there are seven columns and no pediment, but the central column is poised on top of the porch, which was originally an archway. This suggests that at any rate he knew what he was about and the idiosyncrasy was deliberate.

A more subtle feature is the method of dealing with the slope of the ground. The windows step up towards the centre in groups of three (i.e. house by house) while the entablature and string course rise continuously on a gradual slope. This treatment, which Eveleigh also adopted at Somerset Place, succeeds effectively in minimizing the difference in levels.

The elephant crests over the doorways and the coat of arms in the tympanum are those of Charles Pratt, Marquess Camden, who was Recorder of Bath and after whom the Crescent was named. His portrait by Hoare is in the Guildhall.

CAVENDISH CRESCENT [Plan 1 BR13]
John Pinch the elder 1817–30

Cavendish Crescent, just below Somerset Place, is late, small, and plain. There are only eleven houses; there is no central feature and not much decoration; the main accents are the rusticated surrounds to the arched doorways, the handsome frames of the middle first-floor windows of each house, and the prominent string courses and cornice. The wrought-iron balconies are original. Unlike most of Bath's earlier terraces, the third floor forms an integral part of the façade and is not banished to the roof. This is typical of Pinch. The slight change in level is dealt with in the Eveleigh manner by running the string courses and the parapet on the slope and stepping up the windows in groups of three.

CEMETERY CHAPEL, Walcot [Plan 1 CS14]
James Wilson 1842

Bath's burial grounds and their mortuary chapels form an interesting, if gloomy, little field

CAMDEN CRESCENT

of study for connoisseurs of Victoriana. The best known is perhaps the cemetery on the top of Lansdown Hill, within which Beckford's Tower (q.v.), or rather the house at its base, was in use as the chapel from 1847 to 1970. The Romanesque gateway and wall are by Goodridge. Others include the Abbey cemetery on Prior Park Road which was laid out by the landscape gardener J. C. Loudon and has a neo-Norman chapel by Manners (1844); this was intended to have a cloister attached to it which was never built. Adjoining is the Catholic cemetery with a chapel by Charles Hansom who designed St. John's Catholic Church (q.v.) on the South Parade. C. E. Davis's paired French Gothic chapels on the Lower Bristol Road are remarkably successful.

The small original cemetery of St. Swithin, Walcot, across the road below the church, has a neo-Romanesque chapel by James Wilson with

CEMETERY CHAPEL, Walcot

CAVENDISH CRESCENT

the date 1842 over the doorway. This cemetery was closed before 1875.

CHRISTIAN SCIENCE CHURCH, Charlotte Street [Plan 2 EX15]
James Wilson 1845

Built for the Moravians, who had been meeting in their small chapel in Monmouth Street for the previous eighty years. Apparently the congregation were told at the time that their new chapel was a copy of the Temple of Vesta at Tivoli (which is circular). The capitals of the columns do indeed come from this source, but otherwise there is no resemblance. Nevertheless Wilson's façade is a handsome neo-Classical exercise.

This chapel became the property of the Christian Scientists in 1907, when the Moravians built themselves a red brick chapel in Coronation Avenue to the south-west of the city.

• THE CIRCUS [Plan 2 EV16]
John Wood the elder 1754 (see plate on p. 10)

In 1725, at the age of twenty-one, John Wood prepared highly ambitious schemes for the development of two separate areas of Bath. Each of these was to include a Royal Forum, an Imperial Gymnasium, and a 'magnificent Place, for the Exhibition of Sports, to be called the Grand Circus'. One of the two proposed circuses was to have been built in the Abbey Orchard, and this got as far as the drawing-board in 1730, when Wood presented the plans at the opening of Lindsey's Assembly Rooms; but nothing came of this scheme. The Circus to the north-west of the town was not started until 1754, twenty-nine years after Wood formulated his original proposals. Whether after this long interval there was still any lingering intention of using the area for 'the Exhibition of Sports' is highly doubtful to say the least; we certainly hear no more of this after Wood's death, which occurred only three months after he laid the first stone of the King's Circus, as it was then called. Thus he can have had practically nothing to do with the actual construction, which was carried out by his son. But it is always assumed that the design was entirely his responsibility.

The Circus is unquestionably the elder Wood's masterpiece. The use of three entering streets,

CHRISTIAN SCIENCE CHURCH, Charlotte Street
(formerly Moravian Chapel)

rather than the more orthodox four or two, is particularly ingenious, as it means that entering observers from whichever direction receive the impression of a closed circle. Matthew Bramble in Smollett's *Humphrey Clinker* refers to the Circus as 'a pretty bauble: contrived for shew and looks like Vespasian's amphitheatre turned outside in', and many others since, notably Sir John Summerson, have developed this comparison. The amphitheatre (usually called the Colosseum) is vastly larger, as Sir John Soane pointed out in 1809, and it is oval not round, but Wood, who can only have seen it in engravings, may not have appreciated these differences. Although Smollett's reference was intended to be disparaging, there can be no doubt that the resemblance was deliberate, and that the 'theatrical style' of the elevations, to quote a contemporary announcement, was intended to produce an impression of Roman grandeur in spite of the smallness of scale. As in the Colosseum, the scheme consists of three tiers of three-quarter columns, respectively Roman Doric, Ionic and Corinthian, with their appropriate entablatures. These columns are arranged in pairs between the windows; the colonnades run uniformly round the circle without break or variation. The

THE CIRCUS, detail of first-floor frieze

ingenious metopes on the Doric ground-floor frieze are carved with a great variety of subjects; every one appears to be different, although eagle-eyed observers can discover some duplications.

The Circus was originally intended to have 'an equestrian statue of His Majesty' in the centre, but this was never erected and the area was entirely cobbled except for a small covered reservoir. Planting was introduced in the early nineteenth century; and this eventually resulted in the five enormous plane trees which now overtop the buildings. Fierce controversy breaks out periodically about the desirability of their removal. They are certainly picturesque but they obstruct the view and spoil the scale. Compromise of a sort has recently been achieved by sawing off some of the lower branches so that one can at least see the opposite façade through the trunks.

When Mr. Ison wrote his book in 1948 the Circus was in poor condition; the stonework was badly weathered and corroded, the parapets had been altered in ways differing between individual houses, many of the acorns had disappeared, the windows had been cut down at the bases and the glazing bars removed. A painstaking house-by-house restoration has been going on for many years and at the time of writing is almost complete. It has not proved practicable to replace every original feature; for instance the bases of the first-floor windows were originally higher, there were no balconies, and the parapet had no openings. Nevertheless the transformation is little short of miraculous, and this scheme, involving the co-operation and financial support of the

Historic Buildings Council, Bath Corporation and individual house-owners, deserves the highest praise; it is being successfully extended to other parts of Bath, notably Pulteney Street.

CLEVELAND BRIDGE [Plan 1 CS17]
H. E. Goodridge 1827

Originally called the New Bridge, it was renamed after the Duke of Cleveland to whom the Bathwick estate had descended. It remained a toll bridge until 1929, when it was rebuilt, but fortunately the two pairs of neo-Classical toll-houses, with their four-column porticos surmounted by pediments, survive intact.

CLEVELAND BRIDGE, toll house

THE COUNTESS OF HUNTINGDON'S CHAPEL, Vineyards [Plan 2 GV18]
1765

From 1932 Presbyterian, and from 1972 United Reformed Church. A recent writer, leading his readers round Bath, tells them to 'press bravely through [the Paragon] eyes down past the gothicky chapel'. Anyone taking this advice will miss the city's best specimen of early Gothic revival. What one actually sees from the road is not the chapel itself, which is a separate though linked block behind, but Lady Huntingdon's house; later it was occupied by the minister.

Selina Countess of Huntingdon (1707–91) was converted to Methodism by her husband's sister, Lady Margaret Hastings, and was a member of the first Methodist Society founded in London in 1739. After her husband's death she sold her jewels and built a chapel in Brighton, followed by others at Tunbridge Wells and Bath—all fashionable spas; for her 'connexion' was intended to attract members of the aristocracy and upper classes. George Whitefield preached at the opening service of the Bath chapel in 1765. Next year Horace Walpole came to hear John Wesley preach, and wrote a characteristic description: 'My health advances faster than my amusement. However, I have been at one opera, Mr. Wesley's. The chapel is very neat, with true Gothic windows (yet I am not converted); but I was glad to see that luxury is creeping in upon them before persecution: they

COUNTESS OF HUNTINGDON'S CHAPEL,
the manse, Vineyards

COUNTESS OF HUNTINGDON'S CHAPEL,
interior

have very neat mahogany stands for branches, and brackets of the same in taste. At the upper end is a broad *hautpas* of four steps, advancing in the middle: at each end of the broadest part are two of *my* eagles, with red cushions for the parson and clerk. Behind them rise three more steps, in the midst of which is a third eagle for pulpit. Scarlet armed chairs to all three. On either hand, a balcony for elect ladies. The rest of the congregation sit on forms. Wesley is a lean elderly man, fresh-coloured, his hair smoothly combed, but with a *soupçon* of curl at the ends. Wondrous clean, but as evidently an actor as Garrick.'

Walpole called Lady Huntingdon 'the Queen of the Methodists', Whitefield described her as 'all aflame for Jesus', and George III 'wished to God there was a Lady Huntingdon in every diocese in the Kingdom'. But in spite of her virtues she could be dictatorial, and in 1781 she dismissed the minister at Bath for allowing laymen to preach in the chapel; five members of the congregation left with him and set up a Tabernacle in a stable off Monmouth Street.

The little house is a charming piece of Strawberry Hill Gothic, with its battlemented parapet, wide bay, and ogee tops to doors, windows and gates.

THE CROSS BATH [Plan 2 FZ19]
Thomas Baldwin c. 1790

One of the medieval baths of the city which were under the jurisdiction of the bishop and administered by the prior. They passed to the corporation after the Reformation. The Cross Bath derived its name from a cross in the centre which was more than once reconstructed, the last occasion being in 1688 to commemorate the visit of Mary of Modena, James II's Queen, in the previous year. Bathing in this spring was given the credit for enabling her to give birth to a much-desired son. The momentous consequences of this event are well known, and the Cross Bath can thus claim to have altered the course of English history.

The cross was finally removed about 1784 and the bath rebuilt by Baldwin a few years later. He disregarded the medieval lay-out entirely and designed his exterior for the sole purpose of forming an effective termination to his newly built

THE CROSS BATH

Bath Street (q.v.). The plan with its numerous curves is remarkably Baroque for Bath and for its date, but the decoration is purely Baldwin.

The Cross Bath was altered by Palmer in 1798 and again by C. E. Davis in the 1880s. It has since been partially restored, although the blank panels at street level originally held doors and windows,

THE DISPENSARY, Cleveland Place

and the openings on the parapet were filled with stonework carved with swags. There were also festooned vases at each end of this parapet.

THE DISPENSARY, Cleveland Place [Plan 1 CR 20]
H. E. Goodridge 1845 (see plate on p. 61)

Goodridge designed Cleveland Place as an approach to Cleveland Bridge (q.v.) which he built in 1827. It was never completed but has some interesting late Classical façades on both sides. The Dispensary on the east side, somewhat unusual for Bath in being both named and dated, is a pleasant specimen of Goodridge's neo-Classical which goes well with his toll-houses on the bridge. Originally called the Eastern Dispensary—there was a Western Dispensary in Albion Place off the Upper Bristol Road—it had been established in 1832 'to aid with medical advice the sick poor from any parish in or near Bath' and was attended daily by a physician and surgeon.

DORIC HOUSE, Sion Hill [Plan 1   BR21]
Joseph Michael Gandy c. 1805

Built for Thomas Barker, the best known of a Bath family of painters. He was highly successful at his peak, and sold one of his pictures for £500 in 1790. J. M. Gandy (1771–1843), a pupil and protégé of Soane, was more successful as a draughtsman and a painter of architectural fantasies than as an architect. He built nothing else in Bath, and it is not known how he came to receive this particular commission. He exhibited a design for the house at the Royal Academy in 1803. This had a single high storey raised on a plinth and a windowless wall decorated with a frieze behind Doric columns. The executed design modified this somewhat impracticable scheme as will be seen; nevertheless with its blank wall at ground floor level and its antefixes on the roof it is the most uncompromising piece of Greek revival architecture in Bath. Inside there is a gallery thirty feet long originally used for the public display of pictures—an exhibition of paintings 'in the New Picture Gallery on Sion Hill' was advertised in 1805, and the house is shown as 'Barker's Picture Gallery' in a plan of 1813. In 1825 Barker covered one wall of this room with an enormous fresco of *The Massacre of the Inhabitants of Scio by the Turks*, which is still there.

ELIM CHAPEL, Charlotte Street [Plan 2 EX22]
H. E. and A. S. Goodridge 1854

Formerly known as Percy Chapel. It was built

DORIC HOUSE, Sion Hill

ELIM (FORMERLY PERCY) CHAPEL, Charlotte Street

by a breakaway group from the Argyle Chapel, Argyle Street (originally known as the 'Independent Chapel in Laura Place'). The Rev. William Jay had been minister at Argyle for no less than sixty-two years when he retired in 1852. He was an outstanding preacher of national reputation who became known as 'the uncrowned King of the Free Church world'. There was dissension about his successor and Jay was not too old to organize a protest group who formed themselves into a separate congregation. (Incidentally the Argyle Chapel itself had derived from a split-up of the Countess of Huntingdon's Connexion.) Jay died in 1853, but his followers remained in being and built a new chapel the following year; its name was a compliment to Jay who lived for many years in Percy Place.

Pevsner, writing in 1958, calls this 'an awful, spreading Italian Romanesque façade', but tolerance of Victorian eclecticism has gained much ground in the past sixteen years, and this building is now acceptable as, at least, an amiable eccentricity. The architects were H. S. Goodridge, who started as a strict neo-Classicist but turned to Romanesque, and his son A. S. Goodridge. The uninhibited exuberance of this church is mid-century and suggests the hand of the son rather than the father.

EMPIRE HOTEL [Plan 2   HY23]
Charles Edward Davis 1899–1901

Still generally known as the Empire Hotel although it was taken over for offices in 1939 by the Admiralty (now the Ministry of Defence—Navy) who have been in occupation ever since. It calls for inclusion in this Gazetteer as easily the most conspicuous secular building in central Bath; no approval of its architectural merits is implied. Indeed, it has found few friends; apart from any question of design, the way its bulk obtrudes on its neighbours, especially the Abbey, is impossible to defend.

As a large, purpose-built hotel the Empire is contemporaneous with the Midland Hotel, Manchester (Charles Trubshaw 1898); the Russell Hotel, Russell Square, London (C. Fitzroy Doll 1898), described by Pevsner as 'a super-François Premier château with decided borrowings from the Château de Madrid'; the Imperial Hotel (same

EMPIRE HOTEL

square, same architect, also 1898, demolished 1966) 'equally colossal but a much more vicious mixture of Art Nouveau Gothic and Art Nouveau Tudor'; the very French Ritz Hotel, Piccadilly, London (Mewès and Davis 1906) and many others up and down the country. Evidently an era, and an area, in which fanciful architects were given their head by indulgent hotel entrepreneurs. The entrepreneur here was a Mr. Alfred Holland who, in the course of putting his proposals to the Corporation, wrote that he was 'taking it for granted that there are no restrictions as to height'. No one seems to have objected—it may have been relevant that the design was by the City Architect, C. E. Davis. The building which resulted was described as 'Jacobean' at the time and as 'an unbelievable piece of *pompier* architecture' by Pevsner in 1958. The lower five stories are comparatively sober, but perched above these is an astonishing row of doll's houses with little or no relationship either to each other or to the block below. They are, in order, a mock cottage with two bargeboard-and-plaster gables; a curly gable which Sir Nikolaus identifies as 'Loire-style'; and a tower on the angle. Then round the corner a repetition of the Loire façade and the cottage, this time single-gabled. Someone has suggested that these are intended to symbolize the three estates of the realm; as an explanation of the architect's motivation this seems as good as anything. Some balconies have recently been removed from the lower storeys but this has not materially affected the building's appearance.

FRIENDS MEETING HOUSE, York Street,
(formerly Freemasons' Hall)

FREEMASONS' HALL, see Friends Meeting
House

FRIENDS MEETING HOUSE, York Street [Plan 2 GZ24]
William Wilkins 1817-19

Built as the Freemasons' Hall. William Wilkins (1778–1839), the eminent neo-Classical architect whose best-known work is London's National Gallery, also built a new Doric portico to the Lower Assembly Rooms, which were demolished in 1933. This handsome façade is strictly in the Greek taste, although as Ison says the arches over the side entrances are aberrations from the precise canon. The laying of the foundation stone in 1817 and the dedication in 1819 were celebrated with considerable ceremony, the latter in the presence of the Duke of Sussex. The building was used by various Lodges until 1842, when the Rev. J. B. Wallinger, who had seceded from the Church of England, leased the property with some friends 'of the Baptist persuasion', calling it Bethesda Chapel. In 1866 the Society of Friends took over the leasehold, moving from their Meeting House in St. James's Parade. Meanwhile the Freemasons had moved to the old Orchard Street Theatre, which had for a time been a Roman Catholic Chapel—the peregrinations of Bath's congregations can be bewildering to say the least.

NO. 41 GAY STREET [Plan 2 FW25]
John Wood the elder 1740

Gay Street, which links Queen Square to the Circus, was named after Robert Gay, the owner of the land and a prominent London surgeon. It was built at various dates from 1730 until about 1760. Except for two of the houses the elevations are of the standard Bath type of the period. One exception is No. 8, called 'The Carved House' and occupied for a time by Dr. Johnson's friend Mrs. Piozzi, formerly Mrs. Thrale; this has a different and unusually elaborate treatment on the ground and first floors. The other is No. 41. This is the house at the south-east end of the street, at the corner with Old King Street. John Wood took the opportunity of this prominent site facing on to Queen Square to design this elaborate corner bow, rather different in style from his usual work; as Pevsner says, 'Wood's severe Palladianism disappears here, and a heavy but gay Baroque takes

GAY STREET, No. 41

GREAT PULTENEY STREET from Laura Place,
Holburne Museum in background

below his best. His Corinthian pilasters seem "stuck on" to the long façades, at regular intervals but without real significance' (Little); while Ison writes that the two blocks on the north side comprise 'architectural groupings of great length and balanced diversity which the eye cannot possibly take in completely'.

How far are these comments justified? Since Mr. Ison wrote the trees in the street have been cut down, and this, though mourned by many, makes it less difficult to absorb Baldwin's scheme; and the cleaning of the façades, at present in progress, enables the delicacy of the detail to be better appreciated. That there was a carefully worked out scheme, and that the manneristic eccentricities of style are deliberate, cannot be doubted. It must be admitted that the weakness of these façades is their flatness. The width between the buildings is uniform right down the street and the breaks forward are at no point more than a matter of inches. If this is accepted as a limiting factor these frontages can be taken as a courageous attempt to introduce subtle variation, within a Classical idiom, into what would otherwise be a monotonous sequence.

The linking motif through the five terraces of Pulteney Street and the four sides of Laura Place is the repetition at varying intervals of identical fluted Corinthian pilasters; there are nearly a hundred of these altogether. The street is divided into five blocks by three cross-streets, two on the

GREAT PULTENEY STREET, Nos. 18 and 19

its place.' Inside on the ground and first floors there are two oval rooms placed on the diagonal, or more precisely square rooms with semicircular ends in which the bow window is balanced by an internal apse. Their handsome decoration survives.

There is a tradition that this house was designed by the elder Wood for his own occupation, but if this is so it is doubtful when he lived there; he is also said to have designed No. 15 Queen Square for himself in 1730, and he died at No. 24 Queen Square in 1754. But No. 41 is known to have been the town house of the younger Wood.

• GREAT PULTENEY STREET [Plan 1 CS26]
Thomas Baldwin c. 1788

The most important street in Baldwin's ambitiously planned proposals for Bathwick (for which see under Laura Place), and clearly intended to impress. It is long (1,100 feet), wide (100 feet), levelled artificially, designed and built as a co-ordinated whole, and has its vistas effectively closed at one end by Laura Place and at the other by the Sydney Hotel. All the same, Pulteney Street receives only faint praise from modern commentators. Although it has to be accepted as the grandest street in Bath, its detail often comes in for criticism: 'The terraces are very long and not sufficiently, one feels, pulled together' (Pevsner); 'This spacious street is good to walk along and seems Bath's noblest thoroughfare till one studies its elevations. There, however, Baldwin was well

E

GREAT WESTERN RAILWAY VIADUCT

south and one on the north (owing to the non-completion of the estate as planned these cross-streets are severely truncated). The most important block is the centre one on the south side, and this is also the most conventional. It has a large central pediment supported on six of the ubiquitous pilasters and with the Pulteney arms in the tympanum, designed to face down the (unbuilt) cross-street opposite. It also has end features each with four pilasters but no pediments. The major departure from orthodoxy in this group is the addition of two extra pilasters on either side of the central pediment.

The two blocks on the north side are more complicated. They are very nearly identical, and certainly very long; over 120 evenly spaced windows altogether in the two street elevations. Each has four small three-bay pedimented pavilions (the pediment over No. 33 is missing), two at the ends and two framing a central feature consisting simply of a procession of pilasters. The length of these central features is so arranged as to provide for the vistas from the two cross-streets on the south side to be terminated by pediments. A further variation in these façades is that the five bays closest to each end pavilion are framed within paired pilasters, and the centre window of the five has a decorative surround.

The side blocks on the south side have a somewhat similar, though less complicated, scheme. Here the pediments over Nos. 41 and 52 are missing. The most striking eccentricity repeated along these four elevations is the split pilasters cut off by the sides of the pedimented pavilions.

GREAT WESTERN RAILWAY (now British Rail) [Plan 1   CT27]
Isambard Kingdom Brunel 1840

On 31st August 1840, after a race against time to finish the line, the first train reached Bath on Brunel's broad-gauge track from Bristol; the connection to Paddington was not completed until the following year. Construction through Bath was decidedly awkward. The hilly ground meant tunnels and cuttings, notably one through Sydney Gardens, and several roads had to be crossed, some at difficult angles. The placing of the station in a loop of the Avon involved river bridges on the skew at either side; the one on the west extending into a viaduct which also crossed two roads in succession. Architecturally this viaduct is very typical Brunel with its battlemented parapet, turrets with arrow-slits, stepped buttresses and

GREAT WESTERN RAILWAY STATION,
now Bath Spa station

Gothic arches over the footways. The station makes no concession to Bath Classicism; it is Jacobethan with curved gables and tall mullioned-and-transomed windows on the first floor. The asymmetry of the elevation is due to the desire to provide a balanced terminal vista to Manvers Street on which the three gables are centred. This was a new street laid out by the GWR as a continuation of Pierrepont Street and an approach to the station. The curve in the façade to the left of the gables masks the oblique angle between the railway line and the street plan. Originally there was a proper entrance on the south side as well as the north, and a large glass-roofed shed spanning the tracks.

GREEN PARK STATION, Midland Railway

GREEN PARK STATION [Plan 2   EY28]
1869–70

The Bath terminus of the Midland Railway; known for nearly eighty years as Queen Square Station, which must have confused many a visitor to Bath. It was given its more geographically accurate name when the railways were nationalized in 1947–48. It was the end of a spur which joined the Midland's Bristol–Birmingham line at Mangotsfield. In 1874 the Somerset and Dorset Railway was brought into this station, thus providing a link between the south coast and the midlands and north. The architect of this handsome Classical elevation is unknown. Behind it there is a large glass-roofed train shed supported on iron girders reminiscent of St. Pancras, which had been built by W. H. Barlow and F. Ordish for the Midland Railway a few years earlier.

Both lines have been closed for some years and the station has become derelict. It is now the property of the Corporation which has thus been landed, with understandable reluctance, with a conservation problem of major proportions. The train shed is probably irredeemable but there is hope that a way may be found to preserve the fine façade.

GROSVENOR PLACE (originally Grosvenor Hotel) [Plan 1   DR29]
John Eveleigh 1791–c. 1801

Part of a grandiose and never completed scheme for a Vauxhall or pleasure garden of some twenty acres stretching from the river to the London Road, which was to have been surrounded on three sides by 143 houses centred on a hotel. When the foundation stone was laid in June 1791 it was stated that 'pleasure gardens are to be planted next autumn (regardless of expense and opposition) with the utmost exertion of taste and fancy' to include an 'aviary, temple with chimes, labyrinth with merlin swings and cave, grotto, alcoves etc.'.

GROSVENOR PLACE (formerly Grosvenor Hotel)

How much of this ever got off the drawing-board is uncertain, but of the houses only the terrace along the London Road was started and that, with the hotel in the centre, remained unfinished for many years. Indeed, as will be seen, three of the six oval panels between the first and second floors are uncarved to this day. As for the Vauxhall, it proved to be too far out of Bath and too subject to mists from the river, and it never achieved the success of the rival Sydney Gardens.

Pevsner calls the hotel front 'gaily ornate and somewhat vulgar and uninstructed', but Eveleigh was something of a rogue architect and his eccentricities may well have been deliberate. For instance he repeats here the 'solecism' which he perpetrated at Camden Crescent of having an odd number of columns. At Grosvenor this means that the centre column is placed on top of the entrance, originally designed as a wide archway leading into the gardens (the neo-Classical porch is later). The faces carved into the keystones on the ground floor are details which Eveleigh also used at Somerset Place.

The hotel was described as 'now erecting' in 1801, ten years after the laying of the foundation stone, and was commented on as unfinished in 1819. It eventually became a school, then a warehouse; it has recently been converted into flats and the front restored.

• THE GUILDHALL [Plan 2   GY30]
Thomas Baldwin 1776, additions by John McKean Brydon 1891

The long and complicated pre-history of the eighteenth-century rebuilding of the Guildhall was investigated and entertainingly related by Walter Ison in his book in 1948. It starts in 1760 when the Corporation decided 'that the Town Hall be newly built in a more commodious place'. The then existing hall was, according to Wood, 'rebuilt and finished in the Year 1625 after a Draught that was given to the Citizens by Inigo Jones'. Attributions to this architect are often suspect, and the extent of Jones's responsibility for this building is doubtful. The south front was reconstructed about 1737. It was on an island site in the High Street, just north of the Abbey, which had now become too small and an obstruction to traffic. Things moved slowly however, and it was

not until 1763 that the first design for a new Guildhall was commissioned. The architect was Thomas Lightoler (or Lightholder) who at about the same time built the Octagon Chapel in Milsom Street (q.v.). Three more years passed before the Committee decided that this design was too expensive, and invited the younger John Wood, Richard Jones (Ralph Allen's former clerk of works) and Lightoler (again) to submit plans. Wood was paid £30 for his drawings but Lightoler's revised design was accepted, and a year later he was commissioned to make a 'perfect model' of yet another revision. The foundation stone of the new building was laid in February 1768, but things hung fire again until July 1775 when the Corporation decided that 'Mr. Atwood's plan for rebuilding the Town Hall be used accordingly'. Building work seems to have started, rather slowly, at about this time.

This is the first we hear of a design for the Town Hall by Thomas Warr Atwood, but as well as being City Architect he was a member of the Common Council and had been on the Building Committee for the Hall since it was set up in 1763. So it is not surprising that the adoption of his plan led to some cynical comment. This was increased by the submission of a new scheme prepared by John Palmer, the Bath architect, which his business associate Thomas Jelly offered to build at no cost if he was granted a ninety-nine-year lease of the shops and houses included in the proposed layout. This apparently attractive proposition was brusquely rejected by the Corporation. This decision gave rise to a vitriolic and protracted correspondence in the local newspapers in the true tradition of eighteenth-century polemics. Eventually Atwood and Palmer were persuaded to agree to the appointment of an arbitrator in the person of Thomas Paty, the most distinguished of a well-known Bristol family of architects. Paty's decision was strongly in favour of Palmer, but the Corporation took no notice and the controversy continued until cut short by Atwood's death in an accident in November 1775.

Atwood had a young assistant, Thomas Baldwin, who had represented him at the appearance before the arbitrator. Baldwin was an obvious choice to succeed Atwood as the Guildhall architect, and the Corporation commissioned him to

THE GUILDHALL

prepare yet another set of designs which were accepted at the end of 1776. The walls which had already been erected to Atwood's design, but which had reached only fifteen feet high at the most, were pulled down, and building at long last got properly under way.

The Guildhall was Baldwin's first independent work, and it was fortunate for the City that he turned out to have such a high degree of talent; indeed, he eventually proved to be indubitably the most distinguished Bath architect after the Woods. And the Guildhall, 'Bath's noblest public building . . . with the city's best Georgian interior', as Bryan Little rightly describes it, is an astonishing achievement for a young man of twenty-six.

To appreciate Baldwin's Guildhall it is necessary to disentangle it from the considerable additions made by J. M. Brydon from 1891 onwards, the total extent of which greatly exceeds the original building. John McKean Brydon (1840–1901) was a London architect of Scottish origin who had been assistant to Norman Shaw and William Eden Nesfield. His best-known work is his block of government offices in Whitehall. In Bath he also built an extension to the Pump Room (q.v.). Although heavier and more Baroque than Baldwin's Adamesque originals, his work blends in with considerable sympathy and Pevsner calls it a 're- markably successful contribution to the public architecture of Bath'. On the west (High Street) side, Baldwin's Guildhall consisted only of the centre block of five bays without the dome above. This façade survives virtually intact; the glazing bars have recently been replaced. Originally there were single-storey screens masking the markets.

THE GUILDHALL, the ballroom

These were of no great merit and disappeared during the extensions, as did Baldwin's side elevations. But the very fine east front also survives, although, as Ison says, 'partially obscured by a clutter of undistinguished buildings'. Every visitor should penetrate into the councillors' car park to see this. Behind it, approached by the Grand Staircase and filling the whole length of Baldwin's block, is the magnificent Banqueting Hall, by general consent the finest room in Bath. As befits a young architect of 1776, this interior is in the lighter, shallower but livelier style associated with Robert Adam and James Wyatt; the comparison with younger Wood's Assembly Rooms, of eight years earlier, is illuminating.

HOLBURNE OF MENSTRIE MUSEUM
(originally Sydney Hotel) [Plan 1   DS31]
Charles Harcourt Masters 1796, reconstructed by Sir Reginald Blomfield 1913–16

The façade which dramatically closes the vista of Pulteney Street was originally built in 1796, and still presents a superficially Georgian appearance; however, it was so drastically altered in the present century that it is now no more than a hybrid.

HOLBURNE OF MENSTRIE MUSEUM
(originally Sydney Hotel)

The reconstructing architect was Sir Reginald Blomfield (1856–1942) who, as Pevsner puts it, 'added his indispensable touch of the French Dixhuitième' in converting the building to a museum. It was originally built as a hotel, known as Sydney House and forming part of the scheme for laying out as pleasure gardens the hexagonal area of some sixteen acres enclosed by Sydney Place (q.v.). A design for the hotel was prepared in 1794 by Thomas Baldwin. This was only two storeys high and Baldwin probably kept it deliberately low in order to enhance the scale of his Pulteney Street terraces. It was not built and instead the project was carried out by Harcourt Masters, whose elevation was broadly similar but in three storeys. The hotel could only have accommodated a small number of residents and was no doubt more of an eating-house or tavern. There were two tiers of windows behind the portico and no attic storey. The rusticated ground floor extended outwards on each side to the extent of one bay from the main block, but there were no colonnades. On the garden front there was a large projecting segmental loggia, the open first floor of which formed a musicians' gallery. Curving extensions on each side provided a series of alcoves for private parties.

The Sydney pleasure gardens were very successful for a time, but the fashion for this kind of entertainment passed and the building became a hydropathic establishment, and later a school. John Pinch the younger added an attic storey in 1836. It was unoccupied and derelict when bought by the trustees of the museum in 1910. Apart from his alterations to the main façade, Blomfield gutted the interior to provide large galleries on the first and top floors and constructed a totally new elevation to the garden front. This is surprisingly dull and ineffective for so eminent an architect, and it is fortunate that it is well shrouded with trees.

HOLY TRINITY (formerly St. Paul), Monmouth Street [Plan 2   EX32]
Wilson, Willcox and Wilson 1872–74

Occupies part of the site of St. Mary's Chapel, built by Wood 1732–34, after his proposals for the rebuilding of St. Michael's had been turned down by the Vestry, who resented his interference. St. Mary's was the first proprietary chapel in Bath—

there were several others later—and was a fine Classical building with a Roman Doric portico. It was pulled down about 1870 to improve the approach to the Midland Station; a great loss.

The new church of St. Paul was explained at the time it was built as being English Gothic of the latter part of the twelfth century; in 1958 Pevsner called it 'a terrible asymmetrical façade'. Its architects can at least claim credit for courageous exuberance. In the same year, 1872, the same partnership built the Baptist Chapel in Manvers Street (q.v.). The resemblance is obvious, although the chapel is much more subdued.

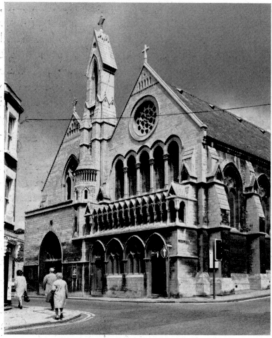

HOLY TRINITY, Monmouth Street
(formerly St. Paul)

THE HOT BATH [Plan 2 FZ33]
John Wood the younger 1775–78

Across the road from the Cross Bath (q.v.). These two and the King's Bath, a short distance away at the other end of Bath Street, were the medieval baths which belonged to the Abbey until the dissolution. After a brief but hectic interlude in private ownership they were handed over to the Corporation. All three were rebuilt in the later eighteenth century and all three, although much altered in the interval, remain essentially Georgian. The Cross and Hot Baths are still in use.

The Hot Bath is the only executed commission which the younger Wood received from the Corporation; he was paid 100 guineas for his services. The building has been much altered but the handsome portico with four Tuscan columns survives basically as he designed it. Originally there was no entrance at this point and the portico shielded a pump from which the public could drink the waters. Inside, the small octagonal central bath, with a band of Pompeian scrolling round the walls, is still recognizable as part of Wood's elaborate symmetrical plan. It now has an iron and glass roof but was originally open and was surrounded by eight dressing rooms, to which there were entrances at all four corners of the building.

THE HOT BATH

KENNET AND AVON CANAL [Plan 1 DT34]
1796–1810

Linked the Avon at Bath with the Kennet, a tributary of the Thames, at Newbury and thus provided through water-communication between Bristol and London. As early as the 1660s four successive Bills were introduced into Parliament for making a water passage between these two towns, but nothing came of them, and it was not until 1788, at the onset of the canal boom, that inaugural meetings were held at which it was resolved 'that the Junction of the Kennett and Avon Rivers will be of Advantage to the Country'. Surveys were made, the great John Rennie reported that there would be no shortage of water, but there was not much financial support until at

KENNET AND AVON CANAL

the end of 1792 Bristol was suddenly bitten with canal fever. Money flowed in quickly for a time, planning progressed more rapidly, an enabling Act was passed in 1794 and construction started the same year. But by 1796 the fever was abating and many of the subscribers, already beginning to have second thoughts, were defaulting on the calls on their shares. Because of this and because, as usual, the cost was far more than had been estimated, work was held up periodically by shortage of funds, and it was not until 1810 that the whole length of the canal was opened.

As with other canals, the Kennet and Avon was reasonably prosperous until the coming of the railways, but suffered a sharp decline after the opening of the Great Western between London and Bristol in 1841. By this time it was a railway fever which was gripping the country, and in 1845 the Committee of Management decided to meet the competition by building its own 'London, Newbury, and Bath Direct Railway' alongside the canal at a cost of £800,000. But this failed to get the necessary parliamentary approval, and in 1851 the Committee was forced to offer the canal to the GWR. Terms were agreed, the necessary Act was passed, and the transfer took place the following year. Business continued to decline under the railway company's administration, the tonnage falling from 360,000 in 1848 to 62,000 in 1905. By 1909 there was already no through commercial traffic on the canal, what there was being confined to local sections. In 1926 the GWR applied to the Minister of Transport for permission to close the whole navigation, but this aroused so much opposition that the proposal was abandoned. But by about 1937 all commercial traffic had virtually ceased. After the war an occasional launch managed to struggle slowly through in spite of weeds, low water levels and damaged locks. The canal was still capable of being navigated throughout when the Railway Executive took over in 1948. Some repairs were done and a loaded barge travelled from Avonmouth to Newbury that year, but the experiment was not repeated. The last through passage from Bristol to Reading was made by the motor launch *Dolly Vardon* in 1951, just before the famous Caen hill flight of locks at Devizes was declared unsafe and closed to traffic. After this, deterioration was

rapid, repairs between Bath and Newbury being limited to work needed to provide a reasonable standard of safety without worrying about navigability. This was in spite of the fact that the British Transport Commission was statutorily obliged to maintain the canal in a navigable condition; in the teeth of opposition, the B.T.C. succeeded in obtaining relief from this obligation in 1956. By this time the Kennet and Avon Canal Association (later Trust) had come into being, pledged to preserve and restore the canal, and it is due to the efforts of this Trust that so much work has been done on the section which goes through Bath. From the junction with the Avon, just south-east of the Spa Station, the canal climbs a flight of seven locks, and passes through Sydney Gardens before leaving the city on the nine-mile pound to Bradford-on-Avon. Near Sydney Gardens it runs through a tunnel under Cleveland House, originally the offices of the Kennet and Avon Canal Company. There is a hole in the roof of this tunnel through which letters were reputedly handed to and from boats passing beneath.

KENSINGTON CHAPEL, London Road

King Edward's School, Broad Street

KENSINGTON CHAPEL, London Road
[Plan 1   DR35]

John Palmer 1795 (see plate on p. 74)

The expansion of building along the London Road in the eighties and nineties meant that by 1795 the new Walcot parish church of St. Swithin's (q.v.), built in 1777, was not large enough for all the residents, and Kensington Chapel was built as a proprietary chapel to provide for the overflow. In 1834 it was bought as a pulpit for the Rev. Edward Tottenham, a popular preacher who was described as the 'Champion of the Protestant Faith'. In 1855 it was let to the Baptists, but by 1917 it was Anglican again and serving as a mission church for St. Saviour's, Larkhall. It has long been disused and neglected, and the interior has been stripped and converted into a warehouse, but the attractive front, which Ison calls 'one of Palmer's ablest designs in the Classic manner', luckily survives almost intact.

KING EDWARD'S SCHOOL, Broad Street
[Plan 2   GW36]

Thomas Jelly 1752 (see plate on p. 75)

In 1742 the elder John Wood was asked to prepare plans for a new building for the City Grammar School, which since 1589 had been housed in the disused church of St. Mary's within the Walls. Wood and the Corporation disagreed about the choice of site and his proposals were rejected. In 1744 the Corporation bought the present site in Broad Street and appointed Jelly as architect, but building did not start until 1752. The well-balanced front shows that Wood was not the only competent architect in Bath. The stone balustrade is modern, but the city arms in the pediment and the five busts are original and by 'Mr. Plura, the statuary' who was paid 41 guineas for his work.

● **LANSDOWN CRESCENT** [Plan 1   CR37]

John Palmer 1789–93

After the Royal Crescent the best-known, the most conspicuous and arguably the most successful of Bath's crescents. The concave-convex-concave-convex sequence of Somerset Place, Lansdown Place West, Lansdown Crescent and Lansdown Place East has been compared to Borromini and

LANSDOWN CRESCENT from the air, with Somerset Place (left) and Cavendish Crescent (below)

even to Art Nouveau: 'This row of houses cuts through the landscape like a whiplash . . . it is an undulating wall, softened in itself, like the one that the illustrator Doudelet invented a hundred years later to illustrate one of Maeterlinck's poems; after 1900, Gaudí also achieved this effect in the terrace of the Güell Park and the façade of the Casa Milà' (Robert Schmutzler, *Art Nouveau*, 1962, p. 54). But Somerset Place (q.v.) was built by a different architect, and its history does not make it likely that it was ever part of a co-ordinated scheme. And as Pevsner points out there are breaks between the two convex wings and the concave crescent which unnecessarily interrupt the sequence. Thus it seems that the serpentine sweep, effective though it certainly is, must be more of a happy accident than a carefully thought-out plan.

Pevsner finds the elevation of Lansdown Crescent 'weak' and the centre 'decidedly awkward and also inadequate. Equally inadequate the two bows at the ends'. Not everyone will go all the way with this rather severe verdict. Whatever its defects, the Crescent creates a handsome and attractive impression; and the problem of providing a satisfactory centre feature, within the Classical idiom, for a curving façade was one which no Bath architect solved entirely satisfactorily. The view over Bath is magnificent, although it is now becoming obstructed, from street level at any rate, by the growth of the trees below. The Crescent is in good condition. Many of the houses have retained their glazing bars or have had them replaced. Only the sliding shutters spoil the façades and these are gradually being taken down. The splendid iron overthrows or lampholders have recently all been uniformly restored by the co-operative enterprise of the houseowners and have had lights installed.

The house at the west end with the bow window was occupied by William Beckford when he sold Fonthill and moved to Bath in 1822. He also owned the adjoining houses on each side and built the connecting bridge to the left. At the back his property reached to the top of the hill where he built his folly (see Beckford's Tower).

LANSDOWN CRESCENT

Lansdown Crescent, overthrow

LAURA PLACE [Plan 2 HX38]
Thomas Baldwin 1788

William Johnstone Pulteney had been intending to develop the Bathwick area, immediately across the weir from the Abbey, ever since his wife Frances inherited the estate in 1764. Progress was slow. The first stage was the construction of Pulteney Bridge (q.v.) which, after protracted negotiations, was begun in 1769 and completed in 1774. Robert Adam, the architect of the bridge, prepared layouts and some elevations for the projected estate between 1777 and 1782, but these were not adopted, possibly due to local prejudice against the employment of a London architect. Instead the planning of Bathwick New Town was entrusted to Baldwin, who was City Surveyor at the time, and building started in 1788. Frances Pulteney had died in 1782, and the estate had been inherited by her daughter Henrietta Laura, later created Countess of Bath. The street names in this area perpetuate various members of the Pulteney family and their successors. The development proceeded rapidly until brought to a sudden halt in 1793, when the failure of the Bath City Bank forced Baldwin and other builder-speculators into bankruptcy. Although some further building was done by the elder John Pinch about 1810, Baldwin's ambitious scheme remains uncompleted to this day, as can be seen by the abrupt terminations of the side streets leading off Pulteney Street.

The planned area starts at Laura Place, which is linked to Pulteney Bridge by the undistinguished and much-altered Argyle Street. Laura Place is a small square on the angle, with a street running diagonally out of each of its four corners. Owing to the differing widths of the streets, the opposite sides of the square are not parallel but this is not very obvious to the observer. The widest and most important of the streets, Great Pulteney Street (q.v.) was completed as planned. Johnstone Street at the south-east corner, what there is of it, was not built until 1805, and Henrietta Street, though built by Baldwin, must surely have been originally intended to run in a straight line at right angles to Pulteney Street instead of curving away to the north as it does.

Placing them out of parallel enables the four elevations of Laura Place to be identical. They tie very closely with those of Pulteney Street and

LAURA PLACE

obviously form part of a single scheme, with the same rather capriciously placed Corinthian pilasters and similar surrounds to the three emphasized first floor windows on each side.

LINLEY HOUSE, No. 1 Pierrepont Place [Plan 2 HZ39]
John Wood the elder 1742

Pierrepont Place forms part of Wood's development of the 1740s south-east of the Abbey and leads off Pierrepont Street through a columned portico. No. 1 has a handsome Ionic doorway surmounted by pineapples, but its main distinction is the splendid plasterwork decoration of two of its rooms. On the first floor the drawing room (used by the Linleys as a music room) has an elaborate ceiling and two shell-headed niches. The ground-floor sitting room has a particularly pretty ceiling with the heads of the four seasons across the corners. The presence of work of such richness in a relatively modest house is explained by the fact that its builder was one John Hutchins, a 'plaisterer'— the original contract of 1742 between him and John Wood survives.

The present name of the house commemorates the residence there in the 1760s of Thomas Linley, the city's leading music teacher, and his talented family. One daughter, Elizabeth Ann, was exceptionally pretty and had a lovely voice. 'Miss

Linley's beauty', wrote Horace Walpole, 'is in the superlative degree. The King admires her and ogles her as much as he dares to do in so holy a place as an oratorio.' George III was not her only admirer. After rejecting an elderly but wealthy suitor favoured by her parents, she was pestered by an adventurer, one Major Matthews, from whom she escaped by eloping to France with the dramatist Richard Brinsley Sheridan. The ensuing complications included two duels between Matthews and Sheridan, and provided the inspiration for the latter's first play *The Rivals*. There is a tradition that while very young Emma Hart, afterwards Lady Hamilton, worked here for the Linleys as a nursemaid.

Linley House is the office of the Bath Festival Society, and the rooms can be seen on application.

LODGE STYLE, Shaft Road, Combe Down [Plan 1 DU40]
Charles F. Annesley Voysey 1909

Originally called St. Winifred's Quarry. The early twentieth century is not Bath's richest architectural period, and it is fortunate that we have even one house by so distinguished an artist.

LINLEY HOUSE, ceiling of ground floor room, *Spring*

LODGE STYLE, Combe Down

Voysey (1857–1941) was a pupil of J. P. Seddon and worked for George Devey and Saxon Snell. He became a prominent member of the Arts and Crafts movement, and Pevsner calls him 'the most important English architect and designer of the generation after Morris'. He designed textiles, wallpaper, furniture and metalwork as well as buildings; his fabrics, which became internationally famous, provided one of the links between Morris and Art Nouveau. As an architect he designed mainly medium-sized country and suburban houses, of which this single storey house built round a courtyard is a typical example.

MANVERS STREET BAPTIST CHAPEL
[Plan 1   CT41]
Wilson and Willcox 1872

Built to replace the chapel in Garrard Street near the Old Bridge, where the Baptists had been meeting since 1768. Their new church was described at the time as 'a good specimen of 13th century work, built in two kinds of Bath stone'. Three years previously the same architects had built the Baptists another chapel in Hay Hill at the upper end of the town, and just at the same time, for the Anglicans, the church of St. Paul, later Holy Trinity (q.v.) in Monmouth Street. Manvers Street, aided by its recent cleaning, is the most acceptable of these three and stands out well among the assortment of modern architecture which surrounds it.

MORAVIAN CHAPEL, see Christian Science Church

NATIONAL WESTMINSTER BANK,
Milsom Street [Plan 2   FW42]
William John Willcox 1865

Milsom Street is basically of the 1760s apart from Somersetshire Buildings (q.v.) of 1782, but was much altered in the nineteenth century, notably and inevitably by the insertion of shop fronts —Jolly's of 1879 is typical. Two Victorian banks frame the street effectively at the George Street end. Ornate and solid-looking, they exude financial rectitude and at the same time present a contemporary interpretation of Bath's Classical idiom. Both buildings are by Willcox and are dated in the stone-work; the National

MANVERS STREET BAPTIST CHAPEL

NATIONAL WESTMINSTER BANK, Milsom Street

Norfolk Crescent

Westminster on the east is 1865 and Lloyds on the west 1875. The earlier is spoilt by the top-heavy attic but is otherwise perhaps the more successful of the two.

NORFOLK CRESCENT [Plan 1 BS43]
1798 onwards (see plate on p. 83)

Norfolk Crescent was apparently named after the Duke of Norfolk; unexecuted plans for the area show also Surrey Street (another of the Duke's titles) and Howard Road (his surname). The Crescent was damaged by bombing in 1942 and was for a long time in a badly run-down condition. Recent restoration by the Corporation has made it possible to appreciate its architectural merits. Ison attributes the design to John Palmer, continued by John Pinch the elder. Building took a long time, as the scheme was initiated in 1792 and only nine of the nineteen houses had been finished by 1810. The façade is very plain, the windows being without architraves or decoration. The only relief, apart from the centre feature, is the ground floor rustication and the pretty iron balconies. As in many of the later Bath terraces, the elevation is four-storeyed. From a practical point of view the additional storey made sense, but it posed problems of design which proved difficult to resolve. Norfolk Crescent has a heavy entablature above the second floor, supported in the centre by six Ionic pilasters, but the crowning pediment is separated from these and perched above the third-floor windows. The effect is not very happy.

At one end of the Crescent is an interesting curiosity, the only remaining watchman's box in the city.

NORTH AND SOUTH PARADES [Plan 2 HZ44]
John Wood the elder 1740–43

Wood had long had his eye on the Abbey Orchard, which lay between the church and the river to the south-east, as a possible development area; and when in 1730 Lindsey's Assembly House was opened with a public breakfast and a ball, he took the opportunity to make a presentation of the plan he had prepared for a Grand Circus on the site—this was twenty-four years before he started to build his Circus on the other side of the town.

NORFOLK CRESCENT, watchman's hut

At first this scheme, which included a bridge over the river, met with approval, but some adverse comment from London discouraged Humphrey Thayer, the lessee of the land, and nothing further happened until after Thayer's death in 1737. The next year Wood was able to secure the land by a 'new Treaty' and altered his plans in order to provide, instead of the Circus, a 'Forum, as the grand Place for publick Assembly'. But now he ran into objections from the Corporation, who were

SOUTH PARADE

before, adding, with no false modesty, that through his works the site had once more become the Glory of Bath.

The Royal Forum got no further in Wood's time, and the 'grand Place for publick Assembly' has long been a car park surrounded by heterogeneous buildings of later periods. The two Parades, with their crossing links Duke Street and Pierrepont Street, are all that was ever constructed of Wood's grandiose plans for this part of Bath; and even here the elevations, owing it would seem to the opposition of the building tenants, were not carried out in accordance with his intentions. These were that the wall supporting the terrace below the Grand Parade should be rusticated and have recesses with arched heads aligned with the windows in the houses above, and a balustrade crowned with obelisks; while the Grand Parade itself would have a centrepiece with Corinthian columns and pilasters. A similar treatment was proposed for the Royal Forum.

After all this, it has to be conceded that the terraces as executed are a disappointment. Although agreeable enough, they are plain and unexciting and a long way from being the Glory of Bath. Moreover, they have been atrociously maltreated by later generations. All the glazing bars have gone; the windows have been cut down at the base and the sill which should run beneath them has been removed; the reveals have been splayed back and painted; ill-fitting iron balconies have been added; the parapets have been mutilated and the stone balustrades replaced by iron railings. The catalogue is endless, and the rash of hotel signs provides a final twentieth-century indignity.

NORTHUMBERLAND BUILDINGS,
Wood Street [Plan 2 FX45]
Thomas Baldwin 1778

This short terrace of seven houses was Baldwin's first venture as a speculative builder. In spite of the delicate detail between the first and second floors the façade is not completely successful. The three meagre pediments, unsupported by pilasters, seem oppressed by the attic storey above. This is apparently original and the block is an early, perhaps the first, example of the four-storeyed terrace elevations which did not become frequent until the following century.

worried about access and drainage; the land, as they bluntly put it, 'appeared little better than an unfathomable Bog'. These difficulties were settled the following year and Wood made a sewer to drain the ground. The year after (1740) he began the building of North Parade, or Grand Parade as it was originally called. Progress was slow and the parallel terrace which Wood intended as the north side of his Royal Forum, later called South Parade, was not started until 1743. This was, he pointed out, on the site of the Priory which had been sold by Henry VIII just two hundred years

OBELISKS [Plans 2 HY46a, 2 FX46b, 1 BS46c]

Bath's three obelisks all commemorate royal visitors. The Prince of Orange came in 1734, benefited from the waters, and gave Beau Nash a gold snuff box. Orange Grove was renamed in his honour and Nash commissioned John Wood to set up an obelisk in its centre. The original intention was that it should be eighty feet high and ten and a half feet square at the base, but more modest ideas prevailed and the executed height was thirty feet. There was a suitable Latin inscription celebrating the Prince's recovery. In his *Essay* Wood estimated the cost of the freestone work at no more than £8 2s. 7½d., and hoped that this 'trifling value' would be 'no small Recommendation to the Building Material of the Hills of Bath for such sort of Ornaments'.

Four years later an obelisk was set up in Queen Square in honour of Frederick Prince of Wales. This was originally seventy feet high and rose to a sharp point, as can be seen in early engravings (the obelisk was damaged in a gale in 1815 and trimmed to its present shape). Again the instigator was Nash and the executant Wood. A model was shown to the Prince, who approved and gave the Beau another snuff box. This model included 'Inrichments' proposed by Wood but not carried out; among these were the Prince's arms, and two lions and two unicorns standing at the four corners of the base. Nash persuaded Alexander Pope to write an inscription for this monument. It has been suggested that Pope was annoyed by the request and deliberately composed the most banal text he could think of. It is certainly decidedly flat, but lapidary inscription is not a field where inspiration strikes to order. The words read: 'In memory of honours conferr'd and in gratitude for benefits bestow'd in this city by His Royal Highness Frederick, Prince of Wales and his Royal Consort, in the year MDCCXXXVIII, this obelisk is erected by Richard Nash, Esq.' Again Wood was very pleased with the low cost, pointing out that 'one of the Egyptian Pillars of this kind, erected by Ramisses, yielded Employ for no less than twenty Thousand Men' whereas the Queen Square obelisk came to only £80 15s. 7d. including the preliminary model. He goes on to drop a strong hint to Mr. Nash about the balance outstanding—apparently the bill for the Orange

NORTHUMBERLAND BUILDINGS

Grove obelisk had still not been finally settled—and to repeat his hope that one or other of the monuments would become 'a Sample to Recommend the Bath Free Stone for its extraordinary Cheapness in Ornaments of this Kind'. The ornament was not universally admired; Malcolm, writing in 1813, calls it 'one of the most disagreeable fancies I have ever seen. This silly Master of Ceremonies might have discovered in the works of the antients, forms far more beautiful than an Egyptian conceived from the rays of the Sun.'

The third obelisk was erected in 1837 and complimented Victoria on the occasion, not as one might guess of her accession to the throne but of her majority a few months earlier—as a member of the royal family she came of age at eighteen. It is in Victoria Park which had been laid out by Edward Davis in 1830 and formally opened by the eleven-year-old Princess, heir-presumptive to the throne, then on a visit to the city with her mother the Duchess of Kent. The obelisk is by G. P. Manners and triangular in plan. This time the lions at the corners of the base were duly executed.

Obelisk, Victoria Park
Obelisk, Orange Grove
Obelisk, Queen Square

THE OCTAGON, Milsom Street

THE OCTAGON CHAPEL, Milsom Street
[Plan 2 GX47]

Thomas Lightoler 1765–67

In the eighteenth century attendance at church on Sunday was of course taken for granted by everyone, visitors and residents alike, and the rapid expansion of the town imposed a serious strain on the available accommodation. One solution was the proprietary chapel, i.e. a privately owned place of worship in which all seats were paid for. In 1732 Wood built the first such chapel in Bath, St. Mary's Queen Square, after he had become concerned about the facilities for his tenants and had failed to come to terms with the Vestry of St. Michael's for the rebuilding of that church. The need was so acute that the news of the proposed construction of St. Mary's immediately increased the demand for house sites in the area, and it is perhaps a little surprising that it was not until 1765 that a second proprietary chapel was built. The Octagon is tucked away behind the houses in Milsom Street. Finance was arranged by the Rev. Dr. Dechair and William Street, a banker—ownership of one of these chapels could be quite profitable—and the architect was Thomas Lightoler (or Lightholder), whose only other known activity in Bath was to submit plans, which were not adopted, for the new Guildhall (q.v.). The new chapel was advertised as 'the only safe place of worship in Bath, with no risk to health as there are no steps to climb and no bodies buried below'. Whether for this reason, or because Herschel was the organist, or because there were alcoves with fireplaces, which Parson Woodforde 'could not think at all decent', the Octagon became the most fashionable church in Bath. In

1783 Mrs. Thrale wrote: 'You will rejoice to hear that I came out alive from the Octagon Chapel, where Ryder, Bishop of Gloucester, preached on behalf of the missionaries to a crowd such as in my long life I never witnessed: we were packed like seeds in a sunflower.'

The interior is approached by a covered passage from Milsom Street. It is, to quote Woodforde again, a 'handsome building, but not like a place of worship' and is even less so now that the organ and double-decker pulpit have been removed. These were at the west end, over the entrance and opposite the small sanctuary, which originally held an altar-piece by William Hoare for which he received £100 and a free seat in the chapel for life. The continuous gallery is, as one might expect, eight-sided and is supported on Ionic columns and surmounted by a shallow dome. The attractive decoration reflects the fact that Lightoler was primarily a carver.

The Octagon remained in use as a chapel until 1895, after which it was for many years an antique showroom. It now belongs to Bath Corporation.

ORANGE GROVE

ORANGE GROVE [Plan 2   HY48]
1706 and 1897 (see plate on p. 89)

The name, and the obelisk in front, commemorate the visit of the Prince of Orange in 1734
(see Obelisks). Originally this was a gabled row of
houses of the transitional early eighteenth-century
type, like the Saracen's Head in Broad Street
(q.v.). The rear wall was probably built up partly
on the wall of the chancel of the Norman abbey.
In 1897 the terrace was given a fanciful new front.
The shell-hoods over every first-floor window
have a certain absurd charm, as has the demi-
turret at the corner with its plaster frieze, balustrade and miniature spire. The glazing bar pattern
is worth noticing. The shop fronts were rebuilt at
the same time and now deserve credit as one of the
tidiest and most uniform in Bath. The contrast
with the disorderly row of shops in Terrace Walk,
just round the corner, is remarkable.

THE PARAGON [Plan 2   GV49]
Thomas Warr Atwood 1768

'The second of Bath's crescents' writes Pevsner.
It is true that the Paragon is curved and that it was
started only eighteen months after the Royal
Crescent. But regarded as an attempt to rival
Wood's masterpiece it is a tremendous anticlimax,
and obviously Atwood, who was an able architect
and astute man of business, cannot have meant it
as such. Looked upon as a crescent, the Paragon
faces the wrong way, that is uphill; lacks a centre
feature; is arguably too long and too shallow; and
above all looks out, not on to an open space, but
on to a row of houses (these are roughly contemporary and were clearly planned to be there from
the start). Simply as one side of a curved street,
however, and this is surely what Atwood intended, the Paragon is remarkably effective; its
length becomes impressive and the shallowness of

THE PARAGON

the curve a positive advantage as it enables the whole extent of the façade to be seen at once. The individual fronts are of the standard Bath type of the 1760s, with doorways framed by Doric pilasters under a pediment, and another pediment over the middle window of each house. The two end houses have a subtle variation in that the ground floor has rusticated stonework with arched openings. The appearance of the terrace would be improved by the restoration of the balustrade with which, Ison says, it was originally crowned.

The Paragon was built on steeply sloping ground, necessitating a huge substructure which gives the back of the block a cliff-like appearance when viewed from Walcot Street below. The houses were planned with the principal rooms at the back to enjoy the view over the river.

PARTIS COLLEGE, Newbridge Hill [Plan 1 AR50]

Samuel and Philip Flood Page 1825–27

Built and endowed under the will of the Rev. Fletcher Partis to provide homes for thirty 'decayed gentlewomen', who had to be over forty, healthy, Anglican, the daughters or widows of clergymen, professional men or others of similar rank, and to have an income of over £25 a year. Each was to receive a pension of £30 a year and be allotted a separate four-roomed house. The Pages seem to have built little else, and indeed practically nothing is known of them except that they were Londoners who occasionally exhibited at the Royal Academy. At Partis College they produced a charming Greek Revival group of three separate ranges round a grass rectangle. Although the word 'College' has no educational significance here, it is not inappropriate as the composition has an academic look reminiscent of, say, Downing College, Cambridge. The middle block has an Ionic portico behind which is the chapel—the College still has its own chaplain, and 'attendance at services is expected twice on Sunday and at least once in the week'.

PARTIS COLLEGE

PERCY CHAPEL, see Elim Chapel

'PINCH'S FOLLY', Bathwick Street [Plan 1 CS51]

This attractive Baroque gateway is something of a mystery. It now leads nowhere but looks as though it was built to adorn an entrance to a gentleman's residence. This is borne out by the coat of arms, now weathered, in the keystone. It is reputed to have been erected in its present position in 1853 by William Pinch, son of the younger John Pinch; his builder's yard was on the land behind. The object, it is said, was to stop coal wagons passing through at this point and force them to use another entrance. It is difficult to believe that this elaborate and no doubt expensive structure was made specifically for so utilitarian a purpose, which could have been served by a few bars of wood or strands of wire. If, as is possible, the gateway was moved from another site, the style seems appropriate to about a century and a half earlier.

'Pinch's Folly' was the subject of one of Leonora Ison's charming decorations for her husband's book. The surmounting urn, which had disappeared, was recently reconstructed in accordance with Mrs. Ison's drawing.

● PRIOR PARK [Plan 1 DU52]
John Wood the elder, completed by Richard Jones 1735–c. 1750

Built for Ralph Allen, the successful man of business (for whose earlier career see under Ralph Allen's Town House). 'Prior Park certainly is a composition in the Grand Manner', writes Pevsner, 'the most ambitious and the most complete re-creation of Palladio's villas on English soil' and no one will disagree with this verdict. So that it is astonishing to find Wood writing that whereas he had prepared a first design in which 'the Orders of Architecture were to shine forth in all their Glory; the Warmth of this Resolution at last abating, an humble Simplicity took place'. Wood also tells us that Prior Park is, in effect, a gigantic builder's sample. In 1726 Ralph Allen bought the quarries at Combe Down south of Bath and began to develop them. The stone although acceptable locally was regarded with disfavour in London, and Allen was disappointed by

'PINCH'S FOLLY', Bathwick Street

the rejection of his tender for the stonework at Greenwich Hospital. This, Wood says, 'brought him to a Resolution to exhibit it in a Seat which he had determined to build for himself near his Works, to much greater Advantage, and in much greater Variety of Uses than it had ever appeared in any other Structure'. To what extent this was Allen's motivation is difficult to decide. As an eighteenth-century tycoon he would inevitably have acquired a large country house sooner or later, but the site of Prior Park was certainly dictated, as Wood says, by its nearness to the quarries.

The two wings have been so much altered and enlarged that Wood's scheme is no longer perceptible, but the splendid exterior of the main house remains much as he left it, except for the stairs on the north front added by Goodridge in about 1830. Although there were originally proposals

Prior Park, the main front

Prior Park, the Palladian Bridge

PRIOR PARK, side elevation
PRIOR PARK, the south (entrance) front

PRIOR PARK, the chapel

for grand external staircases (to a different plan), these were abandoned and apparently there was no entrance on this side of the house before Goodridge's work. This front, looking down the valley towards Widcombe, was clearly designed to impress, with its vast hexastyle Corinthian portico, two columns deep. The south or entrance front is much plainer, with an attached Ionic portico and no surrounds to the windows. The side elevations, five bays wide, are perhaps the most attractive, with central Venetian windows at the first floor level.

The house was gutted by fire in 1836. The only room relatively undamaged, and it was a fortunate survival, was the chapel at the east end (not to be confused with the Catholic Church of St. Paul (q.v.) built in the west wing in 1844). A contemporary account refers to it as 'one of the neatest chapels I ever saw, where the family constantly attend divine service'.

Wood and Allen quarrelled in 1748, and the remaining building work was taken over by Richard Jones, Allen's clerk of works, who spoilt Wood's balanced scheme by altering the design of the east wing. Jones probably built the pretty Palladian Bridge of about 1755, a copy, with variations, of Roger Morris's bridge at Wilton. Purely an eye-catcher, it crosses nothing more significant than a fish-pond.

After the deaths of Allen and his widow, Prior Park was left to his niece Gertrude Warburton, wife of the Bishop of Gloucester. She sold off most of the contents in 1769. On her death the house passed to another niece, Lady Hawarden, whose son sold it to John Thomas, a Bristol Quaker. His heirs sold it to Bishop Baines in 1829, when it became a Catholic seminary and considerable alterations were made to the east and west wings to provide additional accommodation. It has been a boys' school since 1924.

After the fire of 1836 the interior of the house was reconstructed, probably by Goodridge. Just at this time Hunstrete, six miles south-west of Bath, a large house built by Francis Popham in the previous century but never lived in, was being demolished. The material was sold off, and much of this was installed in Prior Park, including a staircase, doors, chimney-pieces, plaster panels and sculpture, all of high quality.

THE PRISON, Grove Street [Plan 2 HW53]
Thomas Warr Atwood 1772–73

In 1765 the City was told of William Pulteney's proposals for his new bridge (Pulteney Bridge, q.v.). As part of the proposed layout the Corporation agreed to let him demolish the old city prison which was in the tower of St. Mary's Church at the North Gate (the nave had been used as the Grammar School until 1752). In exchange, Pulteney provided a site for a new prison on the other side of the river, and commissioned Robert Adam to prepare a design, but the Corporation favoured the city architect T. W. Atwood. The usual delays ensued, and building did not begin until 1772. The new bridge had been started (and presumably the old prison demolished) three years earlier; what was done with the local malefactors in the interval is not recorded.

THE 'NEW' PRISON, Grove Street

The prison has long been disused as such, and was converted into a tenement; at the time of writing it is being renovated. While not of any great distinction in itself, it is an interesting and now rather rare survival and shows that an eighteenth-century prison was designed to look as much as possible like an ordinary house. To appreciate this fully one needs to know that the street level has been lowered, so that what now appears to be the ground floor was originally intended as the basement and would have been concealed. The central arch of the three on the present first floor was the original doorway of the house.

● PULTENEY BRIDGE [Plan 2 HX54]
Robert Adam 1769–74

The only building in Bath by the most fashionable architect of the 1770s, although he prepared designs for the Prison (q.v.) in Grove Street, for new 'Ball and Concert Rooms' (the Assembly Rooms—q.v.) and for layouts for the Bathwick Estate. These were not executed.

The bridge was built for Mr. William Johnstone Pulteney, as he was at the time. Originally William Johnstone, he changed his surname after marrying the heiress Frances Pulteney in 1760. He succeeded to a Scottish baronetcy on the death of his elder brother in 1794. 'Possessed', according to Burke, 'of a considerable estate in America,' he was 'one of the richest subjects in the British empire' when he died in 1805. On the death in 1764 of her cousin William Pulteney, first and last Earl of Bath, Frances Pulteney inherited the Bathwick Estate, i.e. the land immediately over the river from Bath Abbey. If, as her husband planned, this land was to be developed, the sensible thing was to start by linking it to the city by a bridge. The site chosen led to the demolition of, among other buildings, the town prison, which necessitated the erection of a new building

PULTENEY BRIDGE, from the south

elsewhere for this purpose. Pulteney reached agreement with the Corporation about this in June 1765, granting the City the site where the 'New' Prison (q.v.) still stands in what is now Grove Street. But the construction of a bridge required a private Act of Parliament, which caused some delay, and building did not start until 1769.

Pulteney Bridge has shops on it, and this has inevitably inspired comparisons with such similar bridges as the Ponte Vecchio, Florence, the Rialto, Venice and Old London Bridge. Ison suggests that the design may be adapted from a drawing in Palladio's *Terzo Libro dell'Architettura* but the resemblance is not all that close, and Adam would presumably have regarded imitation of Palladio as old-fashioned. There is really no reason to consider this simple but masterly design as anything other than original.

The bridge has been badly mutilated and only the south external front, recently tidied up, gives any idea of its original appearance. And even here the proportion has been spoilt by moving the western pavilion inwards over the arch; and the end porticos of Doric columns have all disappeared. Nevertheless, the view of Pulteney Bridge from Grand Parade is one of the most picturesque in the city.

PULTENEY STREET, see Great Pulteney Street

● THE PUMP ROOM [Plan 2 GY55]
Thomas Baldwin (1786–92), completed by John Palmer (1793–95); extensions by John McKean Brydon (1897) (see plate on p. 23)

As the name indicates, the Pump Room provided comfortable facilities for visitors who wished to drink the waters, a purpose it still serves.

THE PUMP ROOM, colonnade

THE PUMP ROOM, north front

THE PUMP ROOM, extension to north front

An earlier Pump Room was built in 1704–6 by John Harvey. Although described by Wood as 'one of the best Pieces of Architecture the City could boast of, considering the Time when built', it soon proved too small and otherwise inconvenient, and after being enlarged in 1751 it was eventually demolished.

The first part of the present group to be built was the open colonnade across the end of Abbey Churchyard (1786). This has Ionic columns and a pediment decorated with two sphinxes facing a profile of Hygeia within a wreath. The entablature is horizontal and the slight fall in ground level is dealt with by the simple device of making the columns progressively taller from north to south.

The next stage was the building of the low block to the south, then known as the New Private Baths (1788–89), later the entrance to the King's and Queen's Baths. Its façade balanced the colonnade to the north. In 1791 Baldwin started the Great Pump Room. In 1792, before building was completed, he was dismissed by the Corporation and next year John Palmer was appointed in his place. The west front, which was almost certainly designed by Baldwin, links the twin colonnades with a dramatic windowless façade. The ground storey is rusticated, vermiculated and broken only by four huge paterae. Above this there are eight Corinthian columns set in pairs, with three aedicules in the bays between, each of which frames a niche. The north front is less successful; the central pediment and its supporting Corinthian columns have a stuck-on look, and it is not surprising to find that it was originally intended that there should be a projecting portico. This alteration in the plans took place after 1794 and must therefore be due to Palmer, perhaps acting under orders from the Corporation.

It seems likely that Palmer was also responsible for the inside decoration. Although the smallest of the three splendid large interiors in Bath, after Wood's at the Assembly Rooms and Baldwin's at the Guildhall, the Pump Room does not suffer from the comparison. This handsome room with its giant Corinthian columns has a segmental-headed apse at each end. The apse at the east contains a statue of Beau Nash by Prince Hoare above a very fine long-case clock presented by its maker, the great Thomas Tompion, in 1709, both moved from the previous Pump Room, while the other has a pretty serpentine musicians' gallery. The third apse in the south side is a nineteenth-century alteration to take the fountain. The King's Bath, no longer in use but still filled with water, can be seen through the Pump Room windows. This was one of the medieval baths which were administered by the bishop and prior until the dissolution, and then after an interval in private hands passed to the Corporation. It was altered several times and frequently figures in the history of the city, usually in such contexts as overcrowding, uncleanliness, mixed bathing and deplorable behaviour generally.

The extension block on the east side was built in 1897 by Brydon who had made extensive additions to the Guildhall (q.v.) in a similar style a few years earlier. Inside is the Concert Hall; heavier than Palmer's work as one might expect, it is nevertheless a handsome room and the best Victorian interior in Bath. The south colonnade ends in another extension. Originally this was contemporaneous with the Pump Room as is shown by early engravings. It was replaced in 1889 by a little-liked block by C. E. Davis; this has in turn been recently demolished and a new building erected in a careful imitation of Baldwin's style—in the circumstances, a justifiable and indeed admirable piece of pastiche.

- QUEEN SQUARE [Plan 2   FX56]
John Wood the elder 1728–36 (see plate on p. 29)

Apart from its considerable architectural merits, Queen Square is important for two reasons: it was Wood's first operation as a speculative developer, and it was an early, pioneering example of the treatment of a block of houses as a single composition.

As early as 1725 John Wood, then twenty-one years old and working in Yorkshire, had noticed that his native city of Bath was on the verge of expansion, or, as he put it, 'I found Work was likely to go on.' He continued, 'I began to turn my Thoughts towards the Improvement of the City by Building; and for this Purpose I procured a Plan of the Town, which was sent me into Yorkshire, in the Summer of the Year 1725, where I, at my leisure Hours, formed one Design for the

THE PUMP ROOM, interior

Ground, at the North West Corner of the City.' This land belonged to Mr. Robert Gay, a London surgeon and also M.P. for Bath; Wood began negotiations with him in the same year, but it was not until 1728 that the first of several ninety-nine year leases was signed. This enabled work to start on the east side of Queen Square; the whole scheme was completed seven years later.

Although Wood had to make some modifications in his plans from time to time, Queen Square proved to be a success, both architecturally and commercially, with the consequence that it set patterns in both respects for the vast amount of domestic building which went on in Bath over the next hundred years. As the developer, Wood did no building himself. Having obtained leases for the whole area, he subleased sites for individual houses to builders who had to keep strictly to the elevation as laid down by him, but who could vary the interior planning as they, or their clients,

wished. In the 1730s the demand for houses was so great that the builders had no difficulty in finding tenants and obtaining finance from their bankers.

The dominating side of Queen Square is the north, and fortunately it was this side which Wood was able to build exactly as he planned; even more fortunately it survives relatively intact. A recent writer, rebuking Wood for his 'error of use of the classical vocabulary', says that 'the square does not feel like houses at all'. This would of course have been received by Wood as a compliment, for this was precisely the effect he intended. Another commentator, Bryan Little, more percipiently tells us that the 'northern terrace of Queen Square, Bath's most important piece of architecture, has a splendid sense of opulent dignity. It gives to a row of separate houses an impression of monumental unity. A set of lodgings becomes a palace.' Although there was a precedent in the north side of Grosvenor Square, London, which

QUEEN SQUARE, west side

QUEEN SQUARE, south side, doorway

Wood must have seen, the treatment of a group of houses as a single palatial composition was in 1728 very much of an innovation, and an innovation which was followed, frequently and with endless variations, in Bath and elsewhere. (Camden Crescent (q.v.) built by John Eveleigh sixty years later, is a strikingly close copy.) The palace which Wood created out of his seven houses was, as might be expected from its date, very much an orthodox Palladian one, with its large central pediment and end pavilions, Corinthian columns and pilasters, alternate segmental and triangular pediments to the first floor windows, rusticated ground floor—in fact the whole vocabulary. The composition of the square as a whole would have been even more Palladian if Wood had been able to carry out his original intention of levelling the area—this proved too expensive—and treating the east and west sides as supporting pavilions to the central palace. As it was, the square followed the slope of the land; the eastern houses had perforce to be stepped down, and eventually a totally different treatment was adopted for the west side. This consisted of two symmetrical groups of houses with a gap between which formed the forecourt of a large mansion set back from the square. The first occupant of this mansion was Dr. William Oliver, the leading Bath physician of his day, co-founder of the Mineral Water Hospital and inventor of the biscuit which bears his name. It has long since disappeared, and the gap in the

centre of the west side was filled in by the addition of a central block in 1830. This is by the younger Pinch and in the neo-Grecian style of its time. Although handsome enough in itself it is over-large and does not blend well with its Palladian neighbours.

The south side of Queen Square was deliberately designed by Wood on a subdued note as a foil to the north elevation, and was moreover largely destroyed in the last war. Its only features of interest are the exuberant doorways which were probably designed at their discretion by the individual builders of the houses, the restrictions imposed by Wood permitting latitude in these details.

The obelisk in the centre of the square was set up in 1738 by Beau Nash in honour of Frederick Prince of Wales. It was originally sharply pointed and seventy feet high (see Obelisks).

RALPH ALLEN'S TOWN HOUSE, Lilliput Alley [Plan 2 HZ57]
John Wood the elder 1727

Ralph Allen (1694–1764) is one of the great figures of Bath. A very successful man of business, he is generally accepted as being one of the triumvirate responsible for transforming the city into a fashionable spa, the others being Beau Nash and John Wood. He was born in Cornwall, the son of an innkeeper. As a youth he worked in the Post Office in Bath and became Postmaster before he was twenty. This put him in a position to obtain a contract for the cross posts, which, as he was astute enough to realize, could be made very profitable if intelligently reorganized. On this basis he built up a large fortune, which he augmented by the purchase and development of the Combe Down quarries. By 1727 he was sufficiently prosperous to be living in a large house in Lilliput Alley, to which he made additions probably designed by Wood. The house has been swallowed up by accretions of later building, but this fine and elaborate Palladian frontispiece remains, although now only visible through a narrow and cluttered alleyway between Nos. 1 and 2 Terrace Walk. Happily action is being taken to clean the façade and improve the access.

Allen started building his mansion of Prior Park (q.v.) in 1735 and it was ready for occupation

RALPH ALLEN'S TOWN HOUSE, Lilliput Alley

in 1741. The town house also held Allen's business offices and he continued to use the building for this purpose until his death, which explains how he came to construct Sham Castle (q.v.) in 1762 as an eye-catcher from its windows.

REBECCA FOUNTAIN [Plan 2   GY58]
1861

Erected by the Bath Temperance Association, and bearing the wording 'Water is Best' which translates for the benefit of the unclassical the Greek inscription on the Pump Room. It is not distinguished sculpture and the artist is unknown, but Rebecca in the shadow of the Abbey is affectionately looked upon as one of the city's landmarks.

THE REBECCA FOUNTAIN

REGISTER OFFICE, Charlotte Street [Plan 2   EX59]
George Alexander 1841

Charlotte Street has a group of three interesting buildings of the 1840s and 50s: the Register Office, the Christian Science Church next door (q.v.) and the Elim Chapel opposite (q.v.). The Register Office was originally the Bath Savings Bank. It is in an Italian Renaissance style, rather heavy, with a prominent cornice round the top, and is reminiscent of contemporary London clubs such as Barry's Reform.

THE REGISTER OFFICE, Charlotte Street

● THE ROMAN BATHS [Plan 2   GZ60]
(see plate on p. 16)

As this book is about visible architecture and not about archaeology, it seems sensible to confine the entry under this heading mainly to a brief description of what the visitor in 1974 is actually able to see, especially as anyone wishing to be better informed is handsomely provided for. Professor Barry Cunliffe's *Roman Bath Discovered* (London 1971) gives us a full and authoritative account of everything that is known about Roman Bath.

The same author has entirely rewritten the official *Guide to the Roman Remains of Bath* (Bath 1973), which though brief is extremely comprehensive and includes the new excavations of 1971–72.

'The Roman remains at Bath are, with the exception of Hadrian's Wall, the best preserved, most famous and most impressive architectural monuments of the Roman era to be found in Britain.' This is the assessment of Mr. Jon Manchip White, writing the section about Roman Bath in Pevsner's book. 'Yet', he adds, 'we should bear in mind that Bath was not numbered by the Romans among the larger and more important British townships.' The evidence, which is scanty, suggests that the medieval city wall followed the same line as the Roman wall and was built on its foundations. If this is so, the area enclosed by the latter was about twenty-three acres, a quarter the size of the normal Romano-British cantonal capital. There was some overspill but Bath was a small town. Yet it had a magnificent bathing establishment, which makes it clear that its significance was primarily as a spa. This is borne out both by its Roman name of Aquae Sulis, and by the inscriptions on altars and tombstones telling of visitors not only from other parts of Britain but from northern Europe.

The pre-history of Bath and its waters is deeply enshrouded in legend, much of it incredible, and anyone is free to be as sceptical as he likes about the endlessly repeated story of Bladud and his pigs. Nevertheless, the conclusion is unavoidable that these remarkable springs would have been widely renowned long before the Roman invasion, and it is equally certain that their curative powers were recognized and they were endowed with a religious significance. The Romans were credulous about sacred springs and devoted to bathing for its own sake, so it is not surprising to find that a substantial range of buildings, including the Great Bath, came into existence by the end of the first century A.D. During the following 300 years numerous, and complicated, changes were made in the layout, though the Great Bath remained essentially unaltered. The baths were abandoned before the end of the Roman era. There was always liability to flooding—Bath has this trouble to the present day—when the Avon would back up, depositing mud and silt which had to be cleared away. The probability is that after one particularly severe flood no action was taken, and later floods added deepening layers of silt until the whole area reverted to marsh. A protection was thus provided both against the elements and against robbers, which accounts for the survival of lead linings and pipes.

The present entrance is at the north-west corner of the visible complex—there are known to be further baths, as yet inaccessible, to the south and west. Turning left, the visitor has on his right a hypocaust belonging to a tepidarium, or room of tepid heat. The tile pillars supported a floor of stone slabs under which hot air passed. On the left is a small oval swimming bath which was one of the later alterations to the establishment. The visitor now passes into a passageway having on the right the Circular Bath which served as a cold plunge. On the left are two large openings of Roman masonry which now look on the King's Bath but originally provided a view of the sacred spring and beyond it the altar of the temple. The passage leads to the Hall containing the Great Bath. The hall is 110 by 68 feet and the bath 83 by 40 feet at the top; it still has its lead lining, which originally also covered the steps, and its lead inflow pipe. The present superstructure of columns, balustraded gallery and crowning statues is entirely Victorian and bears no relation to the Roman building. The hall was always roofed, originally in timber, but when this was found unsuitable in the steamy atmosphere it was replaced by a brick vault, a section of which can be seen at the west end of the hall.

Beyond the Great Bath is a smaller rectangular bath, known as the Lucas Bath from the name of its discoverer, Dr. Charles Lucas, in the 1760s. Beyond again lie the East Baths, a suite of heated rooms which were several times altered, the floor levels being raised in attempts to avoid flooding.

On the way to the Museum the visitor passes over the Roman culvert, high enough for a man to walk along it, which led to the river. On the left is the actual spring. The doors are modern but the far wall is Roman.

ROSEWELL HOUSE, Kingsmead Square [Plan 2   FY61]
Attributed to John Strahan 1736

The fantastical Baroque decoration of this house, at one time known as 'Londonderry', is unlike anything else in Bath, and also unlike anything else by Strahan, although as Ison points out there are some resemblances of detail with a much plainer house in Queen Charlotte Street, Bristol, which may also be by him. Bryan Little draws attention to the affinity with contemporary houses in South Germany and Austria. Could this be due to the wishes of the owner rather than the archi-tect? He was Thomas Rosewell from Bristol, and his rebus, a rose and a well, appears with the date in a cartouche under the pediment.

The side elevation on Kingsmead Street is in the same style. It seems incredible that the now for-gotten Abercrombie plan of 1945 might have involved the demolition of this house. Fortunately this is no longer likely and the entrance and side fronts have recently been cleaned, although the plate-glass shop windows regrettably remain.

ROSEWELL HOUSE, Kingsmead Square

ROYAL AND ARGYLL HOTELS, Manvers and Dorchester Streets

ROYAL AND ARGYLL HOTELS, Manvers and Dorchester Streets [Plan 1   CT62]
c. 1844

When Brunel's Great Western Station (q.v.) was built in 1840 it stood on open land and access had to be provided. Two streets were laid out for this purpose, Manvers Street running north to join up with Pierrepont Street and, at right angles, Dorchester Street leading to the Old Bridge (now rebuilt as a footbridge). The architect of these near-twin façades on the corners of the two streets is unknown. It seems likely that they were intended as the commencement of terraces running in three directions and providing triumphal approaches to the station. The effect would have been very fine, but the scheme was never carried out and the two blocks stand isolated amid incompatible neighbours mainly of poor quality.

THE ROYAL CRESCENT

The one on the west, recently the Argyll Hotel and earlier the Manvers Arms, is now closed and its future is uncertain.

At one time the Royal Hotel was linked to the station by an overhead footbridge which saved its guests from descending to street level. This was not removed until 1936.

• THE ROYAL CRESCENT [Plan 1   BS63]
John Wood the younger 1767–75

The Royal Crescent is the most dramatic building in Bath, and one of the great set pieces of European architecture. It is the earliest of English crescents, and the culmination of the great town planning scheme of the Woods which started with Queen Square in 1728.

The Royal Crescent differs from its numerous successors in that it is a full semi-ellipse. This means that the two end houses have return frontages along the diameter of the ellipse, which are fully in view of the spectator and are treated as part of the composition. The other crescents are all much shallower and their end returns are normally invisible from the front. There is no doubt that the Royal Crescent gains a feeling of solidity from this difference; the others all seem two-dimensional in comparison. The solidity is increased by the Bernini-esque treatment of the façade as a continuous colonnade of giant columns. Increased perhaps to excess; Pevsner has his doubts about this, commenting '100 columns so closely set and so uniformly carried through are majestic, they are splendid, but they are not domestic'. Certainly this particular treatment was never again attempted for any of Bath's terraces.

The colonnade is not perfectly continuous; in the middle there is the most unobtrusive of breaks, four of the columns being grouped in pairs with a round-headed window between. This method of marking the centre has been variously criticized as being either unnecessary or insufficient. The former view was voiced as early as 1773, as quoted by Ison: 'The wretched attempt to make a centre to the Crescent where none was necessary is absurd and preposterous, in a high degree. The pairing of the pillars is too small a difference to be noted in so large a building, and has led to an egregious solecism, viz., that of placing a window under each pair of pillars. Had the centre been desired, it would surely have been more eligible, as a chapel for divine service was wanted in that part of the town, and is now building but a few yards off, to have made that the centre.'

The Crescent originally faced on to open fields to the south and west. This meant that the normal approach in the eighteenth century would be from the Circus along Brock Street (q.v.), which Wood deliberately kept on a modest scale so as to enhance the dramatic effect of the great sweep suddenly coming into view. This should still be the approach for the modern visitor; it is a missed opportunity to prescribe him a route, as Peter Smithson does, which brings him up from below.

The Crescent has been fortunate in its ambiance. The fields have given way to a green sweep of grass and to Victoria Park, but there has not been the obtrusion of trees which has spoilt the vistas of Queen Square and the Circus. The road is still

No. 1 Royal Crescent, the drawing room

cobbled; Marlborough Buildings at the west end are tactful and modest; and Gilbert Scott's St. Andrew's Church, the spire of which spoilt the skyline, was happily bombed by the Luftwaffe. The usual Victorian mutilations have occurred, including cutting down the bases of all the first floor windows, but this is less noticeable here than elsewhere because they are set back between the columns.

The house at the Brock Street end (No. 1) has recently had its stonework cleaned and repaired, its fenestration correctly restored, its rooms beautifully decorated and furnished, and the whole presented to the Bath Preservation Trust by a generous benefactor. The house is open to the public and affords the only opportunity for the visitor to Bath to see a domestic interior as it would have been in the late eighteenth century.

ROYAL MINERAL WATER HOSPITAL, Upper Borough Walls [Plan 2   GX64]
John Wood the elder 1738–42

Originally called the General Hospital, then the Mineral Water Hospital, the 'Royal' being added in 1887; its present cumbersome official title is the Royal National Hospital for Rheumatic Diseases. The idea of founding a hospital for poor visitors coming to Bath for the cure originated as early as 1716. Over the years subscription lists were opened, plans were prepared and various locations considered and rejected. The site eventually chosen was that of a theatre which had been built in 1705 but had closed down. The prime movers were the triumvirate of Nash, Allen and Wood

THE ROYAL MINERAL WATER HOSPITAL

plus Dr. Oliver, the leading Bath physician of the day. Naturally Wood was the architect. Apart from the top-heavy attic storey added by Palmer about 1793, the façade remains very much as Wood designed it. The chief departure from his intentions is the sculpture in the tympanum, which was to have been a portrayal of the Good Samaritan by Matthyssens, with the inscription 'Go thou and do likewise' on the frieze beneath, where the name of the hospital now stands. This was not executed, but the Good Samaritan eventually made his appearance in the tympanum of the adjoining extension block to the west, built 1859–61 in a conforming style by Manners and Gill. The royal arms in Wood's pediment were not added until the late nineteenth century.

A guide of 1771 gives a 'total Account of Patients relieved, admitted and discharged' from 1742 to 1769, arranged into illuminating categories:

Cured	1,853
Much better	2,773
Incurable	355
Improper	773
Irregular	78
Dead	169

THE ROYAL SCHOOL, Lansdown Road
[Plan 1 CR65]
James Wilson 1856–58

The two big schools on opposite sides of the road up the hill were built by James Wilson in the 1850s in the medieval manner appropriate to Victorian scholasticism, which decreed that a public

The Royal School, Lansdown Road

school should look as much as possible like an Oxford college. As is the way with schools, they have been considerably enlarged since. Kingswood on the west, a Methodist school for boys, derived its name from the suburb of Bristol where it was founded by John Wesley. It moved to Bath in 1852. The style is Tudor, symmetrical, with a square tower and projecting wings, resembling the same architect's Cheltenham College (1841–43).

The school on the east was also built for boys as the Lansdown Proprietary College, but this went bankrupt in 1865 and the buildings were taken over for the Royal School for the Daughters of Army Officers. Architecturally this is much the more interesting of the two and it is perhaps the most noticeably individualistic of Bath's Victorian Gothic buildings. The change from symmetry at Kingswood in 1851 to total asymmetry here five years later, noted by both Pevsner and Little, is striking. Pevsner identifies the style as 'Decorated, handled in a remarkably uncouth way'. The result certainly bears no resemblance to any conceivable fourteenth-century edifice, but

Wilson's eccentricities are clearly deliberate. Are they to be assessed as a lively expression of originality, or as merely perverse? The observer must decide for himself.

ST. JAMES'S PARADE [Plan 1 CT66]
Thomas Jelly and John Palmer 1768

Originally called Thomas Street, this Parade was, as Ison tells us, a private enclave with no wheeled traffic. The genteel picture thus conjured up is very different from the present seedy terraces lining a busy artery. At one time the whole street was under threat of demolition and the north-west corner was in fact sliced off. Hopefully this danger has now receded and there has recently been some renovation, but many of the houses are still very shabby and there are a number of disfiguring shopfronts. The hooded Venetian windows, supported on consoles, are elegant but the chief interest is in the variously treated pedimented doorways. One of these is double with a decorative frieze and curious capitals to the columns.

ST. JAMES'S SQUARE [Plan 1 CS67]
John Palmer 1790–94

Bath, so rich in crescents, is short in squares, and St. James's is the only example approaching Queen Square in scale. In fact it covers nearly the same area; and its treatment is broadly similar with the level north and south fronts forming single compositions and the east and west sides stepping down the hill. It must however be said that in comparison St. James's Square, despite its considerable charm, is far less impressive. One reason for this is that it is not actually a square but a rectangle, with its less interesting east and west fronts nearly half as long again as the north and south. Then the flatter 1790s style of the north side fails to dominate the whole square in the way that Queen Square is dominated by Wood's Palladian façade of sixty years earlier. The end bows are pretty but the central pediment seems too small. Nevertheless, St. James's Square is a pleasant backwater. The arrangement of the four entry streets on the diagonals is unusual, adding to the feeling of enclosure and nowadays presenting a useful discouragement to traffic.

The square was built partly on the garden of Christopher Anstey, the poet who wrote *The*

St. James's Parade, double doorway

ST. JAMES'S SQUARE

New Bath Guide. When he was given notice to
quit in 1790 he expressed his annoyance in the
famous epigram:

> *Ye men of Bath, who stately mansions rear*
> *To wait for tenants from the Lord knows where,*
> *Would you pursue a plan that cannot fail,*
> *Erect a madhouse and enlarge your gaol.*

to which there came the anonymous reply (the
prison was empty at the time):

> *While crowds arrive fast as our streets increase*
> *And the gaol only is an empty space;*
> *While health and ease here court the grave and gay,*
> *Madmen and fools alone will keep away.*

ST. JOHN'S CATHOLIC CHURCH, South Parade [Plan 2   HZ68]
Charles Hansom 1861–67

Hansom was the architect of Clifton College
(1860–80), member of a Victorian family of architects, and brother of the better known J. A. Hansom, who designed Birmingham Town Hall and
invented the 'Patent Safety Cab' which bore his
name. St. John's is described by Pevsner as 'a
demonstrative proof of how intensely the Gothi-

ST. JOHN'S CATHOLIC CHURCH, South Parade

St. Mary, Bathwick

cists hated the Georgian of Bath', and certainly it makes no concession whatsoever to its close proximity to Wood's Parades. But its lofty spire, based on Lincolnshire precedents, has now become an accepted part of the Bath skyline, and its neighbours to the west and south, the car park and the new Police Station, are scarcely entitled to demand any apology.

St. Mary, Bathwick, interior towards west

ST. JOHN'S COURT, see Beau Nash's House

ST. MARY, Bathwick [Plan 1   DS69]
John Pinch the elder 1814–20

One of the earliest, and perhaps the most attractive, of Bath's many Gothic Revival churches. It was originally dedicated to St. Paul,

the intention being to retain the small medieval parish church of St. Mary. But this was on a site close to the river subject to flooding, and was already in a ruinous condition, so that it was demolished in 1815. 'It is to be regretted', reads a comment of 1876, 'that the architect selected late Third Pointed as the style of the building, and still

St. Mary's Buildings, Wells Road

more that the work was executed at a period when the Gothic Revival was in its infancy,' but later taste will count this a blessing. The handsome tower was obviously modelled on that of the Abbey; interestingly it has the pinnacles which were not added to the Abbey until some ten years later. The original interior arrangement had the pews facing west, confronted by a gigantic three-decker with the pulpit and desks for the parish clerk and for the reader 'high above the level of the gallery'. This was swept away in 1866.

Pinch designed a chancel, but this was never built; neither was one designed by Elkington Gill. The actual chancel is of 1873–75 and by G. E. Street, not at his best.

ST. MARY'S BUILDINGS, Wells Road [Plan 1 CT70]

This modest little row is one of the many middle class and artisan terraces which are to be found scattered round Bath within reach of their grander neighbours. Their collective contribution to the Bath scene is enormous, but because they are individually of little architectural importance they have been vulnerable to the developer in a way that the larger terraces could never be. Fortunately this aspect is now coming to be generally realized, and the danger of these minor terraces disappearing one by one is, it may be reasonably hoped, much less than it was a few years ago.

What makes St. Mary's Buildings more than usually noteworthy is the continuous downward sweep of the cornice and string course, linking the houses together with a series of hooked curves. This feature is found elsewhere in Bath, notably in Sydney Place (q.v.) and Cavendish Place (both 1808), where the continuous bands are ornamented; but at St. Mary's, because the slope is

ST. MICHAEL, Broad Street

after the Abbey. As a 'Clerical Historian' wrote in 1864, 'this ambitious structure overtops but does not overpower the venerable Abbey, which appears as she is, the mother of a graceful daughter'. The 'graceful daughter' replaced a church built in 1742 by John Harvey, a stonemason, which had in turn replaced the medieval church of St. Michael-extra-Muros. Harvey's St. Michael was severely criticized by John Wood, largely because his own offer to build a new church had been turned down, but to judge by the drawing in Ison's book it was an attractive building in a Gibbs-like style. It could only seat 500 and by 1812 discussions were already beginning about a larger church, although building did not start until 1835. Manners, then City Architect, is perhaps best known for his drastic restorations at the Abbey; he built several churches in and around Bath, usually in a 'Norman' style, though St. Mark, Lyncombe (1832) is Perpendicular. St. Michael is Early English and his most striking work. Opinions differ as to its merits. Pevsner calls the tower 'crazy' but Bryan Little considers it 'a gracefully pleasing composition' and the church as a whole 'a lovely design'. The basic inspiration is Salisbury Cathedral but the tower and spire are highly individualistic. Manners must get credit for his handling of an awkward site; the ritual east end is at the actual north, bringing the 'west' tower into its dominating position at the point where four roads meet.

ST. PAUL, see Holy Trinity

ST. PAUL, Prior Park [Plan 1   DU72]
Joseph John Scoles 1844 onwards
    Prior Park (q.v.) was purchased by the Catholic Bishop Baines in 1829 to be used as a seminary, and in 1844 the construction of this large church was started in the west wing. From the outside it had the unfortunate effect of unbalancing still further Wood's already mutilated Prior Park composition. But the interior is splendid: 'without any doubt' writes Pevsner 'the most impressive church interior of its date in the county'.
    J. J. Scoles (1798–1863) was the son of a joiner. His parents were Roman Catholics and he was a pupil of Joseph Ireland, a prominent Catholic architect. He built up a large practice in London, mainly in Catholic churches. These were usually

steeper, the curves are much more pronounced. Sydney Place and Cavendish Place are by the elder Pinch, and it seems plausible to suggest that the same architect may be responsible for this modest but well-designed group.

ST. MICHAEL, Broad Street [Plan 2   GX71]
George Philip Manners 1835–37
    The most conspicuous church in central Bath

ST. PAUL'S CATHOLIC CHURCH, Prior Park

Gothic; the best known is the Jesuit church of the Immaculate Conception, Farm Street (1844–49) in a style which Pevsner describes as 'sumptuous neo-Dec-cum-Flamboyant'. St. Paul's is quite different, a Classical basilica with a barrel vault supported on massive Corinthian columns running into an apse.

The church was a long time building. It was continued by Scoles's son after his death and was not formally opened until 1882; but some of the elaborate capitals remain unfinished to this day.

ST. SAVIOUR, Larkhall [Plan 1 DR73]
John Pinch the elder or younger 1829–32

Closely resembles St. Mary, Bathwick by the elder John Pinch, who, Ison suggests, may also

St. Saviour, Larkhall

St. Stephen, Lansdown Road

have designed St. Saviour which was carried out by his son. This is possible as, although the father died in 1827 and building did not start until 1829, plans had been prepared as early as 1824; at that time, however, it was intended that the church should be 'simple and plain in the Doric Order'. St. Saviour omits the Perpendicular panelling of St. Mary and introduces that trade mark of early Gothic Revival the ogee heading to windows and doors. The internal arrangement resembled St. Mary, with galleries round three sides, a short chancel and a three-decker pulpit.

Again as at St. Mary, a new chancel was added to St. Saviour later in the century, in this case in 1882 by C. E. Davis, the City Architect. There is a large, ornate pink-and-white reredos of 1886 by J. D. Sedding, pupil of Morris, Master of the Art Workers' Guild and forerunner of Art Nouveau.

ST. STEPHEN, Lansdown Road [Plan 1 CR74]
James Wilson 1840–45

The much-pinnacled tower of this church half-way up Lansdown hill is a prominent Bath landmark. The congregation ran into trouble as soon as building began because the Bishop, 'finding that the Communion Table, according to the plan selected, would not stand east and west, declared he would not consecrate such a building when completed'. It proved too expensive to alter the plans to comply with the Bishop's requirements, and the church was not in fact consecrated until 1880, presumably by a more tolerant Bishop—it had been licensed as a chapel of ease in the meantime. Two years later the chancel, by Willcox, was added: wide and with a flat ceiling.

Pevsner calls the tower 'crazy', but many people now would consider this a harsh judgement and would agree with Bryan Little in finding it an attractive piece of pre-Pugin Gothic Revival. The interior includes much decoration from the 1880s onwards in subdued arts-and-crafts taste.

ST. SWITHIN, Walcot

ST. SWITHIN, Walcot [Plan 1   CS75]

Thomas Jelly and John Palmer 1777–90

The parish of Walcot originally embraced a considerable area surrounding medieval Bath and its population increased rapidly during the eighteenth century. By 1730 it was the second largest parish in England, and plans were put forward by John Wood and others to replace the existing church. These came to nothing, and it was not until 1777, by which time the population had again greatly expanded, that a new church was built. The *Bath Chronicle* of 19th June of that year stated: 'Sunday se'ennight the Parish Church of Walcot which has lately been rebuilt in a very neat and elegant manner under the direction of Messrs. Jelly and Palmer was opened for Divine Service.'

The body of the church closely resembled that of the same architects' St. James's, built about nine years earlier (gutted in the war and subsequently demolished). It is of a standardized eighteenth-century rectangular pattern, with large round-headed upper windows lighting the galleries, and smaller windows below. The galleries run round three sides of the interior and six Ionic columns support the roof. Jelly and Palmer built no tower at St. James's as the medieval tower was retained until 1848. St. Swithin's tower has a square base surmounted by a circular lantern and a slender spire. It was not finished until 1790.

Inside, the numerous memorial tablets include Fanny Burney (Countess d'Arblay) and John Palmer.

SARACEN'S HEAD, Broad Street [Plan 2 GX76]

1713

Broad Street was a sixteenth and seventeenth-century development, one of the earliest roads beyond the city walls to be built up. It is shown with only four or five buildings in a map of 1572 (Walcot Street was already lined with houses), but it had fifty-six houses by Wood's time. Naturally most of the earlier buildings have been replaced or rebuilt, and the street now presents an interesting

SARACEN'S HEAD, Broad Street

and picturesque medley of dates and styles. The Saracen's Head is one of the two surviving gabled buildings; the other is No. 38 a little higher up. Both are of typical transitional character. The date 1713 is cut into the stonework of this façade which makes it one of the latest of Bath's gabled houses. The dripstones over the second-floor windows are of seventeenth-century type, while the first-floor windows and the quoins are appropriate to the early eighteenth century.

SHAM CASTLE [Plan 1 DS77]
Richard Jones 1762

Perhaps the best known of any of England's eighteenth-century follies, Sham Castle was built for Ralph Allen as an eye-catcher from the windows of his office in Lilliput Alley (see Ralph Allen's Town House). The builder was Richard Jones, Allen's clerk of works who acted as his

architect after he fell out with the elder Wood. The design has been attributed to Sanderson Miller, the amateur architect who rivalled Horace Walpole as a pioneer of the Gothic Revival, and who had constructed a castellated ruin near his own house in Warwickshire as early as 1745.

Sham Castle is still clearly visible from many parts of Bath, but owing to the growth of trees it is not today so outstandingly conspicuous on the skyline as it must have been originally. Mid-nineteenth-century engravings show the walls as considerably more ruinous than they are now, and evidently the castle has been built up since then.

SOMERSET PLACE [Plan 1 BR78]
John Eveleigh 1790–1820

Although it appears to link up with the undulating sequence of Lansdown Crescent (q.v.) and its two wings, Somerset Place is by another architect and the differences in elevational treatment, as well as the rather wide gap of Somerset Lane between the two groups, make it probable that the

SHAM CASTLE
SOMERSET PLACE
SYDNEY PLACE, south range

SOMERSETSHIRE BUILDINGS, Milsom Street

relationship is fortuitous. This is borne out by the history of this crescent; the two centre houses, Ison tells us, were first built as a semi-detached pair and the rest only added later. This accounts for the somewhat noticeable lack of curvature of the façade of these two houses. Nevertheless, they form a very effective and successful centre feature, with the unusual broken pediment and pretty decoration in the tympanum. As at Camden Crescent (q.v.) Eveleigh deals with the change in ground level by stepping down his windows house by house, that is in groups of three, while the cornice and the string course run continuously with the slope. Some of the door keystones form grotesque masks, a detail repeated at Eveleigh's Grosvenor Place (q.v.).

Somerset Place was caught up in the financial crisis of the 1790s and was never finished at the west end. It was badly damaged in the 1942 air raids. In the subsequent reconstruction the opportunity was taken to turn several of the houses into a students' hostel, an ingenious conversion which involved total rebuilding at the back, adding an additional floor, while leaving the front unchanged.

SOMERSETSHIRE BUILDINGS, Milsom Street [Plan 2   FX79]
Thomas Baldwin 1782

Milsom Street was 'developed', as we should now say, by one Daniel Milsom, a wine cooper, from 1761 onwards. But there was a frustrating gap in his planning caused by the presence of the Poor House on the east side. It was not until after 1780 that the site was cleared and a lease granted to Thomas Baldwin, who by then was in business as a speculative builder, and who proceeded to erect the block known originally as Baldwin's

SYDNEY PLACE, porch at east end

Buildings, later as Somersetshire Buildings.

This is not, perhaps, the most likeable group in Bath, but it is noteworthy for three reasons. First, it is extremely elaborate for a row of only five houses; the bowed centre feature and the end pavilions with their fluted Corinthian columns would, one feels, be appropriate on a terrace half as long again. Secondly, it makes no attempt whatever to blend in with the rest of the street; this sort of unneighbourliness is something associated more with the nineteenth than the eighteenth century. Thirdly, although the details are unmistakably Baldwin, the general effect is quite unlike his other work; the contrast with Northumberland Buildings (q.v.), which he built a little earlier, is particularly striking. Could it be that this rather heavy façade was an experiment which he felt was unsuccessful and decided not to repeat?

SOUTH PARADE, see North and South Parades

STATIONS, see Great Western Railway, Green Park Station

SYDNEY HOTEL, see Holburne of Menstrie Museum

SYDNEY PLACE [Plan 1   DS80]
John Pinch the elder 1808 (see plate on p. 123)

The large hexagon of Sydney Gardens was originally intended to have terraces of houses on all sides. Only the two on the arms adjoining Pulteney Street ever got built. The range to the west, Nos. 1 to 14, is of about 1792 and by Baldwin, the architect of the rest of the Bathwick Estate. This is not his best work and although it has some delicate detail it is dull beside the other completed range to the south, Nos. 93 to 103 (the numbering presumably allowed for the unconstructed terraces). This is by the elder Pinch and closely resembles Cavendish Place which was being built at the same time. Both are on the slope and the houses, stepping down the hill, are linked by curves in the entablatures and string courses, an effective device found elsewhere in Bath at this time, noticeably in St. Mary's Buildings, Wells Road (q.v.), Cavendish Place and Raby Place. There is a specially pretty course between the first and second floors decorated with Pompeian scrolling. New Sydney Place, as it was first called, has its centre and ends marked by pediments. As with other four-storeyed elevations such as Northumberland Buildings (q.v.), they do not look altogether happy perched on top of the attic. The arms in the centre are those of the Vanes, the family name of Lord Darlington who then owned the land.

The return front of each end house has two semi-circular bows and a Doric porch. The porch at the upper end is surmounted by a conservatory of the period, charmingly decorated with fanlights and a tent roof with hanging bells.

TERRACE WALK [Plan 2   HZ81]
c. 1750

No. 1, Terrace Walk has the earliest surviving shopfront in Bath, perhaps designed by the elder

TERRACE WALK, shopfront of No. 1

Wood. It is of great charm and remarkably un-spoilt. Although several times painted the stone-work appears to be original. The glazing bars are replacements but in admirable taste; the removal of two bars from each window to accommodate electric signs is a recent misfortune. The four Ionic columns frame three arches, the keystones of which are carved with female heads. The spandrels have decorations, leaf-like at the sides and drapery looped through rings at the centre.

THE THEATRE ROYAL [Plan 2 FY82]
Designed by George Dance the younger, executed by John Palmer 1804–5

There is a tradition, which one would like to believe, that Shakespeare visited Bath with one or other of the touring companies of actors which were driven out of London by the plague in the 1590s. If so, they would have performed in an inn yard or the like, and the earliest permanent theatre

in the city was built by George Trim in 1705 in Borough Walls; this, having already fallen into disuse, was demolished in 1738 to provide the site for the General (later Mineral Water) Hospital. Its successor was in the basement of Simpson's (pre-viously Harrison's) Assembly Rooms in Terrace Walk. Proposals for a new theatre in Orchard Street were advanced by John Hippesley, an actor, in 1747 and plans were prepared by Wood. Al-though opposed, not unnaturally, by the pro-prietors of 'Mr. Simpson's Theatre', the scheme was supported by John Palmer, a wealthy brewer and chandler (not to be confused with John Palmer the architect) and building started in 1749; the architect was not Wood but Thomas Jelly. The Orchard Street Theatre was reconstructed more than once and remained in business until 1805. In 1767 it obtained a licence which entitled it to be called the Theatre Royal, the first in the provinces, and in the later eighteenth century it

THEATRE ROYAL, The Beaufort Square front

was the most important playhouse in the country outside London; amongst other famous performers, Sarah Siddons appeared from 1778 onwards. By 1805 it was clearly too small and awkwardly sited, and a new theatre was built in Beaufort Square. The Orchard Street Theatre became a Roman Catholic Chapel, and for the past hundred years it has been the Freemasons' Hall.

The new building was designed mainly by George Dance the younger. John Palmer executed the work and laid claim to a major share in the design, but Dance's important contribution is made clear from drawings preserved in the Soane Museum. Dance, an eminent London architect and son of the designer of the Mansion House, did no other work in Bath. It is evident from a contemporary description quoted by Ison that in size and in lavish decoration the interior was intended to rival the grandest London theatres. It included four important ceiling paintings by Andrea

Casali brought from Fonthill Splendens, the house built by Alderman Beckford which his son William was just then in process of demolishing to provide stone and funds for his Gothic Abbey. They were taken out of the theatre in 1839, thus escaping the fire, and are now at Dyrham Park. The main front was on Beaufort Square (q.v.) where it somewhat overpowers the modest terraces built by John Strahan eighty years earlier. Originally the ground floor consisted of a uniform arcade of nine arches which included the main entrance to the theatre. The two floors above survive more or less unaltered, though the four lyres on the parapet on each side of the Royal Arms are now eroded beyond recognition.

The interior was gutted by fire in 1862 and rebuilt by C. J. Phipps, who added the present entrance on Sawclose. Although an interesting piece of Victoriana in its way, this addition completely spoils the effect of the handsome Georgian buildings behind and to the right (see Beau Nash's

House) and it ought to be removed (a lorry recently started this desirable operation by demolishing the canopy). Phipps's interior decoration was naturally in the style of the 1860s but the auditorium retains its basic Georgian structure, as can be seen by comparing it with the slightly smaller Theatre Royal at Bristol (1766). These are the largest Georgian playhouses surviving in the country and the only two still in regular use as theatres.

In 1948 Ison wrote that 'The "Grand Front" in Beauford Square, although grimy, neglected and with its crowning ornaments rapidly decaying, is a very precious survival of Dance's work, full of original thought and detailed with Gallic fastidiousness.' The grime, neglect and decay have advanced unabated during the ensuing twenty-five years, but at the time of writing plans are in hand for a restoration following a recent change of ownership. The future of Bath's theatre has been a matter of considerable concern for many years. It is greatly to be hoped that sufficient resources will be forthcoming to maintain and rehabilitate the building and sufficient audiences to ensure its continued use as a theatre.

GENERAL WADE'S HOUSE, Abbey Churchyard [Plan 2   GY83]

c. 1720

The first and second floor façade of this house is one of the few surviving Georgian elevations in the city which antedate Wood, and is, as Ison says, 'probably the earliest example in Bath of the Palladian use of a giant order'. The architect is unknown. The decoration, though striking, is perhaps over-ornate and overcrowded for so small a surface area.

The attic storey is somewhat different in style and may have been added or altered at a later date. The ground floor was converted to an attractive shopfront in the early nineteenth century; this has since been spoilt by the insertion of plate glass.

General, later Field-Marshal, George Wade was M.P. for Bath from 1722 to his death in 1748, and played a prominent role in the life of the city. Amongst other things, he was a close associate of Ralph Allen and may have provided him with financial backing in his early days; he cleared a pathway, known as Wade's Passage or Wade's Alley, through the muddle of houses north of the

THEATRE ROYAL, entrance on Sawclose. Behind and adjoining are Beau Nash's two houses

GENERAL WADE'S HOUSE, Abbey Churchyard

Abbey to make it unnecessary to use the aisle of the church as a short cut; presented a reredos, altar rails and font to the Abbey; and contributed to the eighteenth-century rebuilding of St. Michael's Church, the building of the Bluecoat School and many other good causes.

The next door house on the east side is of about the same date. Ison suggests it may be by Thomas Greenway; the top-heavy third floor is a later addition. The shopfronts in Abbey Churchyard, of varying dates and styles, are well worth looking at.

WALCOT METHODIST CHAPEL [Plan 1 CR84]
William Jenkins 1815–16

The Rev. William Jenkins was an architect who became a minister and who also designed Methodist Chapels at Carver Street, Sheffield (1804) and New Inn Hall Street, Oxford (1817–18). His façade is rather less neo-Classical, and more Methodist-looking, than one of the Bath architects would have made it at the time. The pediment is separated from the entablature by the attic; 'incorrect', as Pevsner says, but a feature found in

ST. MICHAEL'S CHURCH HOUSE, Walcot Street

some of the Bath terraces, e.g. Norfolk Crescent (q.v.). The gate piers are contemporary and originally supported a wrought-iron overthrow holding a lamp.

WALCOT STREET [Plan 2   GW85]

In medieval times Walcot was a separate parish outside the city walls, and Walcot Street is shown lined with houses in a map of 1572. Wood in his *Essay* comments that its position above the Avon makes it 'a noble high Strand' which is 'one of the finest Situations for Building in, that Nature is

WALCOT METHODIST CHAPEL

WALCOT STREET, Nos. 114 and 116, paired shopfront
WALCOT STREET, Nos. 109–119

capable of producing; and sorry I am to say that so charming a Tract of Land should be sacrificed to antient and modern Ignorance; but so it is: For instead of finding it covered with Habitations for the chief Citizens, it is filled, for the most part, with Hovels for the Refuse of the People'. Walcot Street is still a sad medley and no credit to Bath, and the large modern blocks which are starting to go up have so far proved a dubious improvement. There are however a few individual buildings which are worth looking at. St. Michael's Church House on the south side, especially the lettering over the door, is as close to Art Nouveau as anything gets in Bath. There is a very pretty paired shopfront at Nos. 114 and 116; it does seem perverse that, when so many Bath houses have had their ground floors spoilt by being turned into shops, these two should be in use as dwellings. On the other side is an unassuming row of cottages distinguished by the Venetian windows on the first floor.

WIDCOMBE TERRACE

WIDCOMBE CRESCENT AND TERRACE [Plan 1   DT86]
Charles Harcourt Masters c. *1805*

Widcombe Crescent and Terrace, as Ison rightly says, 'together form one of the most

11/9/80

WIDCOMBE CRESCENT

charming minor building ensembles in Bath'. The Crescent is unusual in that its concave front faces uphill, the best rooms being at the back to enjoy the view. The plain elevation of the upper storeys concentrates attention on the elegant paired door-ways under shallow arches, decorated in the lunettes with rosettes and swags. The middle windows over the doors, so placed for symmetry, have to be blind as they are across the party walls of the houses. Widcombe Crescent needs cleaning, but apart from some drain-pipes it is almost en-tirely unspoilt. Perhaps the householders were too poor to pay for the wholesale mutilation of windows that took place all over Bath in the nineteenth century.

Widcombe Terrace is also unusual in that its back doors are on the street and its front doors open on to a paved terrace which bridges the basement of the houses, so that the residents can pass underneath to their gardens on the other side; an arrangement of great originality and charm.

The end facing the Crescent has two rounded bows and urns on the parapet.

WIDCOMBE MANOR HOUSE [Plan 1 DT87] 11/9/80
1727

Although Widcombe is now swallowed up into Bath, it was originally a separate village, and the grouping of parish church and manor house still has a rural feeling to it. The house was rebuilt about 1727 for Philip Bennet, who was M.P. for Bath in 1742 and whose sister married Ralph Allen's brother Philip. The architect is unknown. Mowbray Green suggested that it might be the work of Thomas Greenway, but this attribution is not accepted by Ison; and certainly the design is very sophisticated for a Bath mason of the pre-Wood era such as Greenway. The garden (west) front was refaced in the mid-nineteenth century in the same style; it relates very well, though the bay window is a giveaway. The fountain before

WIDCOMBE MANOR HOUSE

WIDCOMBE CRESCENT, paired doorway

the front door was brought from Italy in the present century. Over the road, and forming part of the manor buildings, are a pretty garden house and dovecote. Widcombe Manor House is fortunate in having had a succession of devoted owners, and although altered from time to time, it has, unlike so many Bath buildings, always been well cared for.

GENERAL WOLFE'S HOUSE, Trim Street
[Plan 2   FX88]
c. *1720* (see plate on p. 25)

Now named after the hero of Quebec who lived here for a time. Trim Street was started in 1707 which puts it at the beginning of the eighteenth-century expansion of Bath, antedating Wood by some twenty years. This small house is a satisfying example of early Palladianism, with its rusticated angles, fluted pilasters and segmental pediments. The military emblems carved in the tympanum are a later addition.

Next door on the left is the arch over John Street called Trim Bridge, or more correctly St. John's Gate. From the description in Wood's *Essay* it sounds as though this was opened up to provide access to Queen Square, i.e. after 1728.

Bath Architects

ᴮATH has always had a strong architectural tradition—some might call it a closed shop—and it is remarkable that a dozen or so of local architects have between them been responsible for at least three-quarters of the important buildings which went up in the city between 1720 and 1914. The balance, with very few exceptions, is split between minor Bathonians such as Harvey, Lightoler and Lowder, and eminent outsiders whose incursions tended to be restricted to one building apiece. The latter group includes Robert Adam, George Dance the younger, William Wilkins, Decimus Burton, G. G. Scott, G. E. Street, J. M. Brydon, C. F. A. Voysey and the two Blomfields, but apart from Adam and Brydon their contributions are not of major significance.

In the brief biographies which follow, buildings included in the Gazetteer are marked *.

ATWOOD, Thomas Warr (died 1775)

Described in his obituary in the *Bath Chronicle* as 'a common-council man of this city, partner in the New Bank, and an eminent plumber'. He was also architect to the city estates and waterworks, which placed him in a position to obtain Corporation leases of land on which he built, as private speculations, *The Paragon on the road to London and Oxford Row on Lansdown Road. This led to comment which came to a head over proposals for a new *Guildhall. In 1775, after fifteen years of procrastination, the Corporation had accepted plans by Atwood and work had started when a rival scheme was put forward by John Palmer (q.v.) and his senior associate Thomas Jelly (q.v.) which appeared to some citizens to be better value financially. A heated and complicated controversy ensued, leading eventually to the appointment of Thomas Paty, a Bristol architect and surveyor, as arbitrator. Paty found for Palmer, but the Corporation paid no attention and the argument continued until Atwood's death in 1775, 'occasioned by the violent contusions he received in the head, etc., by the falling in of the floor of an old house in the market place'. The Guildhall was eventually built by Atwood's assistant, Thomas Baldwin (q.v.).

Atwood's executed buildings included *The Paragon (1768) and Oxford Row (1773) mentioned above, the *Prison, Grove Street (1772–73) and Axford Buildings (1773). Ison suggests that either Atwood or Jelly could have been architect of Bladud (or Bladud's) Buildings (1755) and Milsom Street with the adjoining Edgar Buildings (1761).

BALDWIN, Thomas (1750–1820)

Perhaps the most important eighteenth-century architect in Bath next to the Woods. As a young man Baldwin was clerk and assistant to T. W. Atwood (q.v.) who, when he was killed in an accident in 1775, was City Architect and at the centre of a furious row then raging about the rival plans for the new Guildhall. Baldwin was appointed City Surveyor as Atwood's successor and commissioned to prepare fresh plans for the *Guildhall which were accepted in 1776. His designs for the building mark the transition for Bath from the Palladianism of the Woods towards the lighter style of Robert Adam and James Wyatt. While continuing to hold his city appointment he embarked on speculative building on his own account, especially on the Pulteney Estate at Bathwick, east of the river over Pulteney Bridge. As City Surveyor his chief work after the Guildhall was the *Pump Room (Colonnade 1786, Private Baths 1788, Main Building 1791). He also rebuilt the *Cross Bath in about 1790. He was dismissed by the Corporation in 1792 after failing to comply with an order to deliver up his account books and the Pump Room was finished by John Palmer (q.v.). The national financial crisis of 1793 led to the collapse of the Bath City Bank, which had been backing the Bathwick development, and this in turn forced Baldwin into bankruptcy. However, he continued in private practice as an architect until at least 1813.

His work at Bathwick included Argyle Street (1787), Argyle Chapel (1789, rebuilt and refronted by Goodridge (q.v.) 1821), *Laura Place (1788), *Great Pulteney Street (c. 1788), Bathwick Street (1790), Henrietta Street (1790), the west side of Sydney Place (1792), and Laura Chapel (1795, demolished). Other works in Bath were *Northumberland Buildings, Wood Street (1778), *Somersetshire Buildings, Milsom Street (1782) and *Bath Street (1791). He almost certainly designed the block at the north-west of the Abbey Churchyard (c. 1786) and Nos. 13 to 15 Marlborough Buildings (1790). Ison attributes to him the porch of No. 1 Belmont. In 1794 he prepared designs for the Sydney Hotel in Sydney Gardens, facing down Pulteney Street, but these were not executed and the hotel was eventually built by Charles Harcourt Masters. Outside Bath, Baldwin claimed in 1788 to have 'executed various designs in Wales, Somerset, Wiltshire etc.'; these are untraced except for Hafod House and other work in Cardiganshire for Colonel Thomas Johnes. In 1806 he built the Town Hall at Devizes.

The quantity of Baldwin's surviving work in Bath is considerable, and, while its quality is perhaps uneven, it includes in the Guildhall and the Pump Room two of the finest and most important eighteenth-century public buildings in the city. His reputation as a Bath architect would stand much higher today if it had not been overshadowed by that of the Woods. As Ison writes, 'the sum total of his achievement entitles him to a high place among the minor architects of the eighteenth century'.

DAVIS, Charles Edward (died c. 1904)

Son of Edward Davis. Authors and compilers of indexes often confuse the two Davises, and references to Bath buildings as being 'by Davis' can be difficult to disentangle. Edward Davis was a pupil of Sir John Soane from 1824 to 1826, and became City Architect of Bath. He laid out Victoria Park, 1830 and restored Prior Birde's Chantry in the *Abbey in 1833, publishing a series of engravings

of this Chapel in 1834 (it was re-restored by Sir Gilbert Scott c. 1870). He designed a group of houses in Gothic style on Entry Hill (1828) and Twerton House (1838). Outside Bath he 'violently Normanized' (Pevsner) the church at Marston Bigott, near Frome, in 1844.

Charles Edward Davis, frequently known as Major Davis, also became City Architect. In this capacity he was responsible for preserving the *Roman Baths and making them accessible to the public (1871 onwards). His work as an archaeologist was bitterly attacked in the 1880s, but later criticism has been kinder and Professor Barry Cunliffe, in his authoritative *Roman Bath Discovered* (1971), brings in an indulgent verdict: 'Davis may have been slack in recording his discoveries and he may have obscured much by covering the remains with cumbersome and inelegant structures, but a wealth of information remains unscathed beneath his floors and will in time be available for further examination.' As an antiquarian he was responsible in 1857 for the recognition, and thus indirectly for the restoration, of the small but important Saxon church of St. Lawrence at Bradford-on-Avon. This building, its origins totally unknown, was being used as a school.

As an architect and restorer the younger Davis has come in for a good deal of criticism from later generations. His block at the south-west corner of the Pump Room (1889) has recently been demolished without regrets. Ison describes his alterations at the Cross Bath (1880s) as 'vandalism', his additions to the New Private Baths (1886) as 'vulgar' and 'ridiculous', and his modernization of the interior of the Pump Room (1888, since removed) as 'disastrous'. His church work included the rebuilding of most of All Saints, Dunkerton (1858–60), the drastic restoration of the chancel of St. Nicholas, Bathampton (c. 1865), the reredos at St. Matthew, Widcombe (c. 1870), enlarging St. John the Evangelist, Weston (c. 1870), another drastic restoration at St. Mary Magdalene, Langridge (1872), the new St. Peter's Church on the Lower Bristol Road (1878–80) and adding the chancel to *St. Saviour, Larkhall (1882). He built the quite attractive Gothic cemetery chapel off the Lower Bristol Road (1862), the remarkable Italianate drinking fountain in Ladymead (1860) and the Market House, Trowbridge, also Italianate

(1861). In 1871 he refaced the block on the north side of Quiet Street opposite the Bazaar. But by far his most conspicuous contribution to the Bath scene, late in his career, is the overwhelming *Empire Hotel (1899–1901), challenging the Abbey with its extraordinary skyline. This time it is Pevsner who uses the word 'disastrous', and asks 'what can have gone on in the mind of the designing architect?'

EVELEIGH, John

With Baldwin and Palmer one of the three most prominent Bath architects of the late eighteenth century. Of obscure and probably humble origins, he first appears as an assistant to Baldwin in the 1780s. As was not unusual, he combined the careers of architect, building speculator and builders' merchant. In an advertisement in the *Bath Chronicle* in January 1790 he offers for sale 'Chimney Pieces' and 'Patent Water Closets' ('which may be fixed in any parlour, bed or dressing room, without the least effluvia'); offers to contract for copper roofing; and, almost as an afterthought, adds: 'N.B.—Designs for Mansions, Villas, Dwellings, etc., executed in the Gothick or modern taste. Buildings superintended, estates surveyed, rents collected, etc.'

In 1793 he was bankrupted by the failure of the Bath City Bank, as was Baldwin. Apparently he then left Bath, and designed the new 'Gothick' Guildhall in Plymouth in 1800.

In Bath his major works were Bailbrook Lodge, Batheaston (c. 1786), *Camden Crescent (1788), *Somerset Place (1790–1820) and *Grosvenor Place (1791). He also built The Mall, Clifton, Bristol (1788).

Ison comments that Eveleigh 'used a curiously personal idiom, successfully fusing elements drawn from Baroque and Adam sources. Although they undoubtedly possess many features which might offend the purist, his designs for Grosvenor and Somerset Place have a vigorous and original quality which lifts them far above the general level achieved by pattern-book architects.'

GILL, John Elkington (died c. 1874)

Mainly recorded as partner of G. P. Manners (q.v.), but on his own he prepared plans for a chancel for *St. Mary, Bathwick in 1870. These were not adopted; the vicar, 'feeling the necessity of dealing with so important a building in a larger and more complete manner', sent to London for G. E. Street. Gill restored the church of St. John Baptist, Hinton Charterhouse and restored and partly rebuilt the parish church of Holy Trinity, Bradford-on-Avon (1864).

GOODRIDGE, Henry Edmund (died 1863)

Son of James Goodridge, a builder who carried out much of the later work in Bathwick. H. E. Goodridge was in practice in Bath by 1819; exhibited at the Royal Academy from 1828 to 1848; and had as his assistant from 1834 to 1838 H. L. Elmes, later the designer of St. George's Hall, Liverpool. His son, Alfred S. Goodridge, worked with him and continued his practice after his death.

Pevsner says of his design for *Beckford's Tower, Lansdown (1823–27) that it 'characterizes the change from Grecian to Victorian' and this phrase aptly summarizes Goodridge's career as a whole. His neo-Classical works include the new front to the Argyle Chapel (1821), the High Street entrance to the Corridor (1825), *Cleveland Bridge (1827), the *Dispensary, Cleveland Place (1845) and the Roman Catholic Pro-Cathedral, Clifton, Bristol (1839). The Lansdown Tower is also Classical, in a way, but is really in a style of its own. The (old) Chapel at Downside School (1823), St. Michael, Atworth, Wiltshire (1832), Holy Trinity, Combe Down (1832–35) and Holy Trinity, Frome (1837) are Gothic, and he added the west window to Malmesbury Abbey in 1830. The wall and gates screening the Cemetery which now surrounds Beckford's Tower are 1848 and Romanesque, as is *Elim Chapel (formerly Percy Chapel), Charlotte Street (1854, with A. S. Goodridge). He also built the staircase on the north front at *Prior Park (c. 1830), and was probably responsible for the reconstruction of the interior of this house after the fire of 1836. Ison attributes to him the attractive front of *'The Bazaar', Quiet Street, built in 1824.

GREENWAY, Thomas

He was primarily a mason, with a yard at Widcombe. His sons Benjamin and Daniel were employed by Wood as 'carvers and vase-makers' on the Exchange, Bristol (1741). Wood's *Essay* mentions him as the builder of the Cold Bath House, Widcombe and St. John's Court, Sawclose. The Cold Bath House (c. 1707) has been completely demolished; Ison described it as 'one of the earliest examples in Bath to show a competent use of Renaissance detail'. The houses called St. John's Court survive, much altered (see *Beau Nash's House). No other buildings can be definitely ascribed to Greenway, although Ison considers he may have been responsible for No. 15, Abbey Churchyard, next to *General Wade's House. Mowbray Green's attribution of *Widcombe Manor House is not always accepted.

Although evidence is lacking, it seems likely that there was a connection with the Greenways of Mangotsfield and Bristol, masons and architects. The most famous member of this family was Francis Howard Greenway (1777–1837), who began as an architect in Bristol, went bankrupt, was sentenced to death for forgery, reprieved and transported to Australia, where he had a second career as the first architect of any merit to work in Sydney.

JELLY, Thomas

At a period when a dividing line between builders and architects barely existed, Jelly was primarily a builder who was capable of producing a competent design. This is proved by the one surviving building he is definitely known to have designed without an associate, *King Edward's School in Broad Street (1752). He also built the Kingston Baths (1763–66); these were demolished from 1878 onwards in order to open up the Roman Baths. As a builder he was associated with Thomas Palmer, a glazier and the father of John Palmer (q.v.). The younger Palmer became Jelly's partner and together they put up proposals for a new *Guildhall in 1775, which were not accepted; they rebuilt the nave of St. James's Church in 1768–69 (demolished); built *St. Swithin's Church, Walcot in 1777, and probably *St. James's Parade in 1768. Ison attributes to Jelly the theatre in Orchard Street (1749, since greatly altered and now the Freemasons' Hall) and thinks that he may have had a hand in the design, as well as the construction, of a number of Bath terraces, such as Gallaway's Buildings (1742–50), Bladud Buildings (1755), and Milsom Street (c. 1763).

KILLIGREW, William

One of the artisan-architects of the generation immediately preceding Wood. The latter condescendingly describes him as 'a Joiner, who laid his Apron aside about the year 1719', and says of Killigrew's setting-out at St. John's Hospital that he 'took such a false Survey of the Land, that there is scarce a Right Angle in the whole Building'. Killigrew's recorded works are few, and the only one which survives, the chapel of St. John's Hospital, has been altered practically out of recognition. He added a ballroom to Harrison's Rooms, Terrace Walk, in 1720; built Weymouth House (destroyed 1942) and No. 3 St. James's Street South at about that time—these two were behind St. James's Church, roughly where Woolworth's now stands. He built the original Bluecoat School in the Sawclose in 1722. The attractive house in St. James's Street South, deplorably demolished only a few years ago, was typical of Killigrew's transitional style. It had a symmetrical front of five bays and four storeys, the centre windows on the first and second floors being framed with fluted pilasters over an elaborate doorway. The attic floor was surmounted by two shallow gables; these were not functional and were half-way to being pediments. The elevations of Weymouth House and the Bluecoat School had marked similarities to this house.

MANNERS, George Philip

A prolific Bath architect of the period 1820–60. Early in his career he was in partnership with Charles Harcourt, previously Charles Harcourt Masters (q.v.). He became City Architect, and about 1845 took J. Elkington Gill (q.v.) as his partner. As City Architect he was responsible for the first, somewhat ruthless restoration of the *Abbey (1824–33) and for altering the *Hot Baths to Decimus Burton's designs (1830). His churches included *St. Michael, Broad Street (1835–37) and the Catholic Apostolic ('Irvingite') Church, Guinea Lane (1840, small and Romanesque). He built the chapel in the Abbey cemetery off Prior Park Road, also Romanesque (1844), the *Obelisk in the Victoria Park (1837) and Twerton Gaol (1843). Outside Bath he built Holy Trinity, Godney (1839), All Saints, East Huntspill (1839), and Holy Trinity, Cleeve (1840), all in Somerset, and Christ Church, Bearfield, near Bradford-on-Avon (1841). The Manners and Gill firm built St. Matthew, Widcombe (1846–47), the tower and the west end of St. James's Church, since demolished (1848), the offices of the Bath Gas Light and Coke Company in Upper Bristol Road (1858–59), and the new *Bluecoat School (1860). They added considerable extensions to both the *Royal Mineral Water Hospital (1850–60) and the United Hospital (c. 1860). Outside Bath they altered Christ Church, Frome (1851) and St. Mary, Kingston Deverill, Wiltshire (1846) and built Emmanuel Church, Weston-super-Mare (1847).

MASTERS, Charles Harcourt

Chiefly known as a surveyor. He drew road maps for the Bath Turnpike Trust in 1786–87, and a plan of Bath which was published in 1794. This had originally been made to enable him to construct a model of the city to the scale of thirty feet to the inch, which he exhibited at his house in Orchard Street in 1789–90 and later in London. A rival model, Ison tells us, was made by a competitor which was not only on the larger scale of twenty-four feet to the inch but had real water flowing in the Avon.

Architecturally, Masters's main work was the Sydney Hotel, now the *Holburne Museum (1796). He also built *Widcombe Crescent and Terrace (c. 1805) and Bloomfield Crescent (c. 1807). About 1807 he changed his name to Harcourt, and later he took G. P. Manners (q.v.) into partnership.

PALMER, John (1738–1817)

Son of Thomas Palmer, a prosperous glazier associated with Thomas Jelly, builder and architect (q.v.), John Palmer began his career as Jelly's partner, and together they rebuilt the nave of St. James's Church (1768–69) in a basically classic style with some Gothic trimmings. (This church was altered by Manners and Gill in 1848, gutted in the raids of 1942 and has since been demolished.) In 1775 the partners put forward a scheme for the rebuilding of the *Guildhall in competition with the proposals of the City Architect, Thomas Warr Atwood (q.v.). Although the Jelly and Palmer

plan had many advantages, financial and otherwise, it was brusquely rejected by the Corporation. This led to a heated public controversy which ended only with Atwood's sudden death in an accident in November 1775. In the event the Guildhall was built to new designs by Thomas Baldwin (q.v.), Atwood's assistant.

In 1792 Palmer was appointed City Architect in succession to Baldwin, who had been dismissed following his repeated failure to comply with an order to deliver up his account books. As a consequence Palmer took over the completion of the *Pump Room which Baldwin had begun in 1791. Attribution of this building as between the two architects (and possibly others) is not totally clear; Ison considers that Palmer had no hand in the exterior design but was responsible for the interior of the Great Pump Room.

Other works by or attributed to him are *St. James's Parade (1768, with Thomas Jelly); the reconstruction in 1775 of the old Theatre in Orchard Street (now much altered and the Freemasons' Hall); *St. Swithin's Church, Walcot (1777–90, with Thomas Jelly); *Lansdown Crescent (1789–93); *St. James's Square (1790–94); All Saints' Chapel, Lansdown (1788–94, demolished); Kensington Place and Percy Place, London Road (1795–98); *Kensington Chapel (1795, disused); Unitarian Church, Trim Street (1795, altered 1860); Christ Church, Montpelier Row (1795–98); Seymour Street (1792–96, demolished); Green Park Buildings (1799–1808, continued by Pinch); *Norfolk Crescent (c. 1798); and the new *Theatre Royal, Beaufort Square, to designs by George Dance junior (1804–5, interior rebuilt after a fire 1862).

Palmer was a prolific architect, especially in the 1790s. 'His buildings', Ison comments, 'while lacking the stamp of an original mind, are distinguished by sober good taste and excellent craftsmanship'; and Lansdown Crescent with its attendant wings is second only to the Royal Crescent as the most splendidly impressive of Bath's terraces.

John Palmer should not be confused with his namesake, a 'wealthy brewer and chandler' who promoted the Orchard Street theatre in 1749, nor with the latter's son, also John Palmer, the postal reformer.

PINCH, John, the elder (1769–1827)

The leading Bath architect of the first quarter of the nineteenth century. He built the south range of *Sydney Place (1808), Cavendish Place (1808–16) and Raby Place, Bathwick (c. 1825). These terraces are on the slope and the houses are linked by curved downsweeps in the entablatures and string courses, an effective device characteristic of this architect. He also built *Cavendish Crescent (1817–30), Sion Hill Place (c. 1820) and part of Park Street. Ison thinks it almost certain that he built Winifred's Dale, a bow-windowed semi-detached pair of villas below Cavendish Crescent. He probably had much to do with *Norfolk Crescent and with the later streets in Bathwick such as Daniel Street and Darlington Street. Apart from domestic architecture, he built the United Hospital in Beau Street (1824–26) (now the Technical College), a somewhat heavy Classical composition made heavier by the attic storey added by Manners and Gill about 1860. *St. Mary, Bathwick (1814–20) is a charming exercise in 'incorrect' pre-Pugin Gothic Revival. Ison suggests that the rather similar *St. Saviour, Larkhall may have been designed by the elder Pinch, although it was carried out by his son after his death.

PINCH, John, the younger (died 1849)

He was the son of the elder John Pinch and worked as his father's assistant, succeeding to his practice at his death in 1827. Earlier, in 1823, he had designed a Gothic Revival house called The Nunnery in the Isle of Man for General Goldie-Taubman, whose wife described him in her diary as 'a very intelligent young man . . . a very clever Architect in the Gothic style especially—the Father and Son built two beautiful new Churches, the Houses in New Sidney Place and some Gentlemen's Seats'. *St. Mary, Bathwick must be one of the churches, but no other church as early as 1823 and no 'Gentlemen's Seats' are recorded for either father or son.

In Bath Pinch built the neo-Classical centre block on the west side of *Queen Square (1830) between Wood's two blocks of a hundred years earlier, and he added an attic storey to the Sydney Hotel (now *Holburne of Menstrie Museum) in 1836. His other recorded works are all churches and usually Perpendicular, although St. John Baptist, Farrington Gurney (1843) is neo-Norman. The first was *St. Saviour, Larkhall (1829–32) possibly to his father's designs. He rebuilt three churches on to existing towers: St. John Baptist, Midsomer Norton (1830, chancel and Lady Chapel added in the present century); All Saints, Upper Weston on the outskirts of Bath (1832, chancel and transepts rebuilt 1893); and Holy Trinity, Paulton (1839). He also built Christ Church, Stratton-on-the-Fosse (1837–8, with a later chancel).

STRAHAN, John (died c. 1740)

A contemporary of John Wood the elder, who describes how, about 1726, 'one John Strahan came to Bristol; and, by printed Bills, offering his Service to the Publick, as a Land Surveyor and Architect, Mr. Hobbs, the Deal Merchant thereupon took him under his Patronage, and employed him in laying out some Meadow and Garden Ground on the West Side of the Body of the City of Bath into Streets for Building'. The 'streets for building' included Avon Street, which has been totally rebuilt, *Beaufort Square (at first called Beaufort Buildings) and Kingsmead Square in which stands *Rosewell House, which has a Baroque elevation of great originality which is unique in Bath. Wood called Beaufort Buildings 'Piratical Architecture'; the justification for the abusive adjective is not too clear, but evidently there was bitter rivalry between the two men.

Strahan was mainly a Bristol architect. The one surviving building which he is definitely known to have designed is Redland Court on the northern outskirts of that city (1735). In a guide of 1781 he was said to have built 'many other capital mansions in and near Bristol'. None of these has been identified, though Frampton Court, Gloucestershire (1731–3), Earnshill, Somerset (1726–31) and Combe Hay, also Somerset (c. 1730) all resemble Redland. He was responsible for a fine Baroque organ gallery in stone at the west end of St. Mary Redcliffe, swept away by the Victorians, and almost certainly for two houses in Prince Street, Bristol, built about 1726 for the timber merchant John Hobbs whom Wood mentions. He was formerly credited with Redland Chapel but Ison, in his book on Bristol, shows that this was most probably designed by William Halfpenny.

WILSON, James (1816–1900)

A leading Bath architect of the period 1840–85, at first alone and later with a succession of partners. Among his churches were the Moravian Chapel (1844–45, now *Christian Science Church), neo-Classical, and *St. Stephen, Lansdown (1840–45), Gothic, with a fine tower which is a conspicuous Bath landmark. He was the architect of Cheltenham College (1841–43) and of both Kingswood School (1851) and the *Royal School (1856–58). He also built the Walcot Schools on Guinea Lane, a massive Italianate block on an irregular, steeply sloping site. Outside Bath he built or rebuilt churches at Shipham, Uphill, Redhill and Norton Malreward, all in north Somerset.

His best-known partner was William John Willcox, who came to Bath in 1865 on winning a competition for the Grand Pump Room Hotel (demolished 1960); his design was in a Classical style appropriate to Bath but with the addition of a massive French-looking roof. Willcox built the *National Westminster and Lloyds Banks in Milsom Street and added the chancel to St. Stephen in 1882. Outside Bath he did much work in South Wales and rebuilt St. Nicholas, Radstock in 1879. Wilson and Willcox together built two Baptist chapels, Hay Hill (1869) and *Manvers Street (1872), and with Wilson's son, J. B. Wilson, St. Paul (now *Holy Trinity) Monmouth Street (1872–74).

Another of Wilson's partners for a brief period was Thomas Fuller (1822–98). Fuller emigrated to Canada in 1856 with another Bath architect, F. W. Stent (born 1822) after winning the competition for the Dominion Parliament Buildings at Ottawa with a Gothic design of the Gilbert Scott type. Before he left Fuller had designed the Town Hall at Bradford-on-Avon (1855).

WOOD, John, the elder (1704–54)

The Woods, father and son, are certainly the most important and most famous of Bath architects and town developers, and theirs is the only name which is likely to be found in general architectural histories and reference books.

The elder Wood was for long believed to be a Yorkshireman, apparently on the grounds that he was known to have been at work there at an early age. However it has now been established that he was born in Bath and educated at the Bluecoat School. There is no record of when he left Bath, or why, but at about the age of sixteen he was already working as a surveyor on the elaborate formal lay-out of the gardens at Bramham Park, near Leeds, a house recently built by Lord Bingley. A little later Wood was working in London, almost certainly brought there by Bingley who had acquired a large, probably uncompleted, house in Cavendish Square designed by Thomas Archer for Lord Harcourt in 1722. He worked also for other patrons, notably the Duke of Chandos who became his first client in Bath. His London experience was of considerable importance to Wood. In matters of design he gained a sound knowledge of the fashionable Palladian idiom from such buildings as Colen Campbell's houses in Old Burlington Street, and as to town-planning he was strongly influenced by the development then proceeding on the Grosvenor and Harley estates, each of which was being laid out as a self-contained district centred on a large square.

The turning point in Wood's life occurred in 1725 while he was dividing his time between Yorkshire and London. He had heard, doubtless from his family, about a new Act of Parliament for paving and lighting the Bath streets, and also about proposals for making the river Avon navigable between Bristol and Bath. This caused him, in his own words, to 'begin to turn his thoughts towards the Improvement of the City by Building'. He sent home for a plan, and, as he wrote later in a much quoted passage from his *Essay towards a Description of Bath*, 'formed one Design for the Ground, at the North West Corner of the City; and another for the Land, on the North East Side of the Town and River. In each Design, I proposed to make a grand Place of Assembly, to be called the Royal Forum of Bath; another Place, no less magnificent, for the Exhibition of Sports, to be called the Grand Circus; and a third Place, of equal State with either of the former, for the Practice of medicinal Exercises, to be called the Imperial Gymnasium of the City, from a Work of that Kind, taking its Rise at first in Bath, during the Time of the Roman Emperors.' He laid these proposals before the respective landowners, Mr. Gay, a London surgeon, and the Earl of Essex. Although Wood's wording is not clear on the point, it seems likely that the two schemes were alternatives and there was never any intention that there should be two forums, two circuses and two gymnasiums. Even one such 'Design' would have proved wildly impractical if Wood's proposals had been taken literally; and in the event, of course, neither was realized to the full. There was no response from Lord Essex, but Mr. Gay was interested at first, only to get cold feet when the death of George I in 1727 caused a political crisis. Meantime Wood had undertaken his first Bath commission, a group of houses for the Duke of Chandos, and had moved to the city. Although Gay was no longer willing to enter into a partnership arrangement he was prepared to lease some of his land; and so Wood took what must have been the momentous step of embarking on speculative development on his own account, starting with the east side of *Queen Square. This was a financial success and Wood's career was assured. A little later he built Lindsey's (afterwards Wiltshire's) Assembly Rooms for Humphrey Thayer and the adjoining part of Terrace Walk, both since demolished. In 1732 he built St. Mary's Chapel at the corner of Queen Square. *Gay Street was started about 1730, and in 1735 he began Ralph Allen's great Palladian mansion of *Prior Park—earlier he had altered *Allen's town house in Lilliput Alley. Wood was one of the prime movers in the proposals for a new hospital which after many years of discussion eventually started building in Upper Borough Walls in 1738 (later called the *Royal Mineral Water Hospital). In 1740 his plans for a 'Royal Forum' in the area south-east of the Abbey got under way after many difficulties and delays—they were never fully realized (see *North and South Parades). In the neighbourhood of Bath he built Belcombe Brook Villa, near Bradford-on-Avon, now called Belcombe Court (1734), and Titan Barrow, Bathford (1748). He built a new Classical cathedral at Llandaff (1734-36, demolished 1844), and the Exchanges at Liverpool (1749-54, much altered since) and Bristol (1741-43), which is arguably the best eighteenth-century building in that city. In Bath his last and finest work was the *Circus, begun shortly before his death and completed by his son.

Wood wrote several books, of which by far the most important is *An Essay towards a Description of Bath*, published in 1742, revised in 1749 and re-issued in 1765. The *Essay* is badly organized, egocentric, idiosyncratic and sometimes downright crazy, as when it purports to describe the University of the Druids at Stanton Drew; but to this day it continues to be required reading for anyone seriously interested in Bath's history.

WOOD, John, the younger (1727-81)

Son of the elder John Wood, and his successor as Bath's leading architect and developer. 'The finest achievements of the son surpass those of the father,' writes Ison, 'both in breadth of conception and subtlety of realization. In fact, the work of the younger Wood represents the highest point of the Palladian achievement in Bath.' This is even more true, if, as is possible, he had some share in the design of the *Circus, the foundation stone of which was laid by his father in 1754 only three months before he died 'from a long and tedious illness'. Anyway, he alone was responsible for the brilliant modification of his father's intended layout which resulted in the *Royal Crescent (1767-75) perhaps the most architecturally famous terrace of houses in the world. His other major work, the *Assembly Rooms (1768-71) is poorly placed and externally rather subdued, but the suite inside is magnificent. The *Hot Bath (1775-78) was his only municipal commission, although he prepared designs for the *Guildhall which were not executed. His other work in Bath was confined to the development of the streets in the area near the Circus and Crescent: *Brock Street (1767-68) with Margaret Chapel behind the north side, *Alfred, Bennett, Russel and Rivers Streets of the early 1770s and Catharine Place (c. 1780). The façades of many of these houses show variations due to the individual builders for which Wood was not responsible.

Outside Bath he built Kelston Park, Somerset (1770) and designed a reredos in 1760 for Bitton church just over the Gloucestershire border. In Wiltshire he added wings to Standlynch, later Trafalgar House (1766) and built the General Infirmary at Salisbury (1767-71, much added to later) and the pretty church at Hardenhuish, near Chippenham (1779). In 1781 he published *A Series of Plans for Cottages or Habitations of the Labourer*.

Short Bibliography

THE literature of Bath is enormous, and no comprehensive bibliography exists. All that can be attempted here is a brief selection of works of architectural interest.

Three books call for special mention. John Wood's *An Essay towards the Description of Bath* (1742 and 1749), has been lavishly drawn upon by many subsequent writers—perhaps too lavishly, for Wood is not very reliable except for his own lifetime. But this book has been highly influential and is still worth reading; it is now available in a Kingsmead reprint. Walter Ison's *The Georgian Buildings of Bath* (1948, reprinted 1969) is the essential source-book for its period; thoroughly researched, well illustrated and definitive. Pevsner's *North Somerset and Bristol* in the *Buildings of England* series (1958) fills in the pre- and post-Ison eras and adds Sir Nikolaus's inimitably pungent and witty comments; quotation is irresistible even, or indeed especially, when one disagrees.

Apollo, November 1973, special issue on 'Bath in the Eighteenth Century'

BALL, Adrian, *Yesterday in Bath*, 1972

BRITTON, John, *The History and Antiquities of Bath Abbey Church*, 1825; revised edition with additions and some omissions by R. E. M. Peach, 1887

CLEW, Kenneth R., *The Kennet and Avon Canal*, 1968

COARD, Peter, *Vanishing Bath*, 1972

COLLINSON, John, *The History and Antiquities of the County of Somerset*, 1791

COLVIN, H. M., *Biographical Dictionary of English Architects 1660–1840*, 1954

CUNLIFFE, Barry, *Roman Bath Discovered*, 1971

FERGUSSON, Adam, *The Sack of Bath*, 1973

GADD, David, *Georgian Summer*, 1972

GREEN, Mowbray A., *The Eighteenth Century Architecture of Bath*, 1904

HADDON, John, *Bath*, 1973

LITTLE, Bryan, *The Building of Bath*, 1947

LITTLE, Bryan, *Bath Portrait*, third edition 1972

MAINWARING, R., *Annals of Bath 1800–34*, 1837

MASON, Roger, *Bath Aquae Sulis*, 1973

MEEHAN, J. F., *Famous Houses of Bath and District* and *More Famous Houses of Bath and District*, 1901 and 1906

PEACH, R. E. M., *Rambles about Bath*, seventh edition 1876

SMITH, R. A. L., *Bath*, second edition 1945

SMITHSON, Peter, *Bath: Walks within the Walls*, 1971

STONE, Barbara, *Bath Millenium: The Christian Movement 973–1973*, 1973

SUMMERSON, John, *Heavenly Mansions*, 1949

WARNER, Richard, *The History of Bath*, 1801

—and various guides, pamphlets and articles in journals

Index

*(Main entries are in **bold** type, illustrations in italics)*

Abbey, 9, 20, 21, 22, 27, 31, **41–8**, 117, 118, 130, 139: *41, 42, 43, 45, 46*; Norman Abbey, 42–3; Saxon Abbey, 42

Abbey Church House (formerly Hetling House), 27

Abbey Churchyard, 20–1, 28, 128–30, 137, 139

Abbey Green, 27, **48**: *48, 49*

Abercrombie Plan, 107

Adam, Robert, architect, 30, 49, 80, 96, 97–8, 136

Alexander, George, architect, 105

Alfred Street, **48–9**, 143: *49*

All Saints, Upper Weston, 141

All Saints' Chapel, Lansdown, 140

Allen, Philip, 133

Allen, Ralph, entrepreneur, 14, 24, 28, 92–6, 103–5, 110, 123, 128; town house, Lilliput Alley, **103–4**, 143: *104*

Anne, Queen, 28

Anstey, Christopher, poet, 112–14

Aquae Sulis, 9, 16, 106

Archer, Thomas, architect, 142

Argyle Chapel, Argyle Street, 63, 137, 138

Argyle Street, 80, 137

Argyll Hotel, **108–9**: *108*

Assembly Rooms: 'New' or 'Upper' 30, 31, **49–51**, 97, 99, 143: *50, 51*; 'Lower' (Harrison's or Simpson's), Terrace Walk, 49, 64, 126; Lindsey's (afterwards Wiltshire's), Terrace Walk, 58, 84, 143

Atwood, Thomas Warr, architect, 68–70, 90–1, 96–7, **136**, 140

Atworth, Wiltshire, St. Michael, 138

Austen, Jane, 9, 14

Avon Street, 141

Axford Buildings, 136

Bailbrook Lodge, Batheaston, 138

Baines, Bishop, 96, 118

Baldwin, Thomas, architect, 30, 51–2, 61–2, 65–6, 68–71, 80, 85, 98–100, 124–5, **136–7**

Baldwin's Buildings (later Somersetshire Buildings), Milsom Street, 124

Ballance Street, 33

Barker, Thomas, painter, 62

Barlow, W. H., architect, 67

Bath City Bank, 80, 137, 138

Bath, Countess of, *see* Pulteney, Henrietta Laura

Bath, Earl of, *see* Pulteney, William

Bath Gas Company, offices, Upper Bristol Road, 140

Bath Preservation Trust, 48, 110

Bath Savings Bank, Charlotte Street (now Register Office), **105**: *105*

Bath Street, **51–2**, 137: *12*

Bath Temperance Association, 105

Bath Turnpike Trust, 140

Bathampton, St. Nicholas, 137

Bathford, Titan Barrow, 143

Bathwick Estate ('Bathwick New Town'), 30, 59, 65, 80, 136–7

Bathwick Hill, 11, 31

Bathwick Street, 137

'The Bazaar', Quiet Street, **52**, 138: *52*

Bearfield, Wiltshire, Christ Church, 140

Beau Nash's House, Sawclose, **52–3**: *52*

Beaufort Hotel, 20

Beaufort Square (originally Beaufort Buildings), 20, **53**, 127, 141: *53*

Beckford, Alderman, 127

Beckford, William, 48, 53–4, 78, 127

Beckford's Tower, Lansdown, 20, 31, **53–4**, 57, 138: *53*

Belcombe Brook Villa (now Belcombe Court), near Bradford-on-Avon, 143

Bellot, Thomas, 45

Belmont, No. 1, 137

Bennet, Philip, 133

Bennett Street, 48, 50, 143

Bilberry Lane, 27

Bingley, Lord, 142

Birde, William, Prior of Bath, 44; chantry 47, 137

Bladud Buildings, 136, 139

Bladud, Prince, 16, 106

Blomfield, Sir Arthur William, architect, 136

Blomfield, Sir Reginald, architect, 71, 136

Bloomfield Crescent, 140

Bluecoat School, Sawclose, 31, **54–5**, 130, 139, 140, 142: *32*

Bradford-on-Avon, Holy Trinity, 138; St. Lawrence, 137; Town Hall, 142

Bramham Park, near Leeds, 142

Bridewell Lane, 27

Bristol: Exchange, 30, 138, 143; Prince Street, 141; Queen Charlotte Street, 107; Redland Chapel, 141; Redland Court, 141; St. Mary Redcliffe, 141; Theatre Royal, 128; *see also* Clifton

Britton, John, 41

Broad Street, 11, 28, 121–3

Brock Street, 18, 19, 30, **55**, 109, 143: *19, 54, 55*

Brunel, Isambard Kingdom, engineer and architect, 9, 13, 66–7

Brydon, John McKean, architect, 31, 70, 98, 100, 136

Burghley, Lord, 45

Burney, Fanny, 121

Burton, Decimus, architect, 136, 139

Camden, Charles Pratt, Marquess, 56

Camden Crescent, **55–6**, 68, 103, 124, 138: *56*

Campbell, Colen, 142

'The Carved House', Gay Street, 64

Casali, Andrea, artist, 127

Catharine Place, 143

Catherine of Braganza, Queen, 28

Cavendish Crescent, **56**, 141: *57, 76*

Cavendish Place, 117, 125, 141

Cemetery Chapels, **56–8**, 137, 139: *57*

Chandos, Duke of, 29, 142, 143

Chapman, Peter, 45

Charles II, 16

Chaucer, Geoffrey, 27

Cheap Street, 27

Cheltenham College, 112, 142

Christ Church, Montpelier Row, 140

Christian Science Church, Charlotte Street (formerly Moravian Chapel), 31, **58**, 105: *58*

Church Street, 19

Circus, 18, 30, 31, 55, **58–9**, 109, 143: *10, 19, 59*

Claverton, 24

Cleeve, Somerset, Holy Trinity, 139

Cleveland Bridge, **59**, 62, 138: *59*

Cleveland, Duke of, 59

Cleveland House, 13, 74

Cleveland Place, 62, 138

Clifton, Bristol: The Mall, 138; Roman Catholic Pro-Cathedral, 138

Cold Bath House, Widcombe, 139

Combe Down Quarries, 28, 92, 103

Combe Hay, Somerset, Manor House, 141

Cook, Ernest, 51

The Corridor, High Street, 138

The Crescent, *see* Royal Crescent

Cross Bath, 27, 52, **61–2**, 72, 136, 137: *61*

Cunliffe, Professor Barry, 105–6, 137

Cure, William, mason, 48

Dance, George, the younger, architect, 126–8, 136, 140

Daniel Street, Bathwick, 141

Darlington, Lord, 125

Darlington Street, Bathwick, 141

Davis, Charles Edward, architect, 31, 57, 61, 63, 100, 120, **137–8**

Davis, Edward, architect, 47, 86, **137**

Dechair, Rev. Dr., 89

Devey, George, architect, 82

Devizes, Town Hall, 137

di Costello, Adrian, 44

Dispensary, Cleveland Place, **62**: *61*

Doll, C. Fitzroy, architect, 63

Dorchester Street, 108

Doric House, Sion Hill, 31, **62**: *62*

Downside School, 138

Duke Street, 85

Dunkerton, Somerset, All Saints, 137

Dyrham Park, Gloucestershire, 127

Earnshill, Somerset, 141

East Huntspill, Somerset, All Saints, 139

Edgar, King of England, 42

Edgar Buildings, 136

Edney, William, smith, 48

Elim Chapel (formerly Percy Chapel), Charlotte Street, **62–3**, 105, 138: *62*

Elizabeth I, 45

Elmes, Harvey Lonsdale, architect, 138

Empire Hotel, 9, 13, 31, **63**, 138: *63*

Entry Hill, 137

Essex, Earl of, 143

Ethiopia, Emperor of, 14

Eveleigh, John, architect, 30, 55–6, 67–8, 103, 123–4, **138**

Farrington Gurney, Somerset, St. John Baptist, 141

Fisher, Martin, architect, 33

Fonthill, Wiltshire, 53, 78, 127

Forum Cinema, 33

Foxhill, 13

Frampton, Sir George, sculptor, 44

Frampton Court, Gloucestershire, 141

Frederick, Prince of Wales, 86, 103

Freemasons' Hall, Orchard Street (formerly Theatre), 127, 140; York Street, *see* Friends Meeting House

Friends Meeting House, York Street, 31, **64**: *64*

Frome, Somerset, Christ Church, 140; Holy Trinity, 138

Fuller, Thomas, architect, 142

Gahagan, Lucius, sculptor, 52

Gallaway's Buildings, 139

Gandy, Joseph Michael, architect, 31, 62

Garbett, William, architect, 47

'Garrick's Head', 53

Gay, Robert, surgeon and land-owner, 29, 64, 102, 142–3

Gay Street, **64**, 143: *64*

General Hospital, *see* Royal Mineral Water Hospital

George III, 61, 81

George Street, 82

Gill, John Elkington, architect, 54, 111, 117, **138**, 139, 141

Godney, Somerset, Holy Trinity, 139

Goodridge, Alfred S., architect, 62–3, 138

Goodridge, Henry Edmund, architect, 31, 52, 53–4, 57, 59, 62–3, 92, 96, 137, **138**

Goodridge, James, builder, 138

Grammar school, 76

Grand Parade 9, 98; *see also* North Parade

Grand Pump Room Hotel, 31, 142

The 'Grapes', Westgate Street, 27

Great Pulteney Street, **65–6**, 71, 80, 137: *65*

Great Western Railway **66–7**, 74; Spa Station, 9, 13, 66–7, 74, 108: *66*

Green, Mowbray A., architect and historian, 51, 133, 139

Green Park Buildings, 140

Green Park Station, **67**, 72: *67*

Green Street, 28

Greenway, Francis Howard, architect, 139

Greenway, Thomas, mason and architect, 28, 52–3, 130, 133, **138**

Greenwich Hospital, 92

Grosvenor Place (earlier Grosvenor Hotel), 56, **67–8**, 124, 138: *67*

Guildhall, 30, 31, 51, **68–71**, 99, 100, 136, 139, 143: *69, 70*; old Guildhall, 68

Hafod House, Cardiganshire, 137

Hamilton, Duchess of, 54

Hansom, Charles, architect, 57, 114

Harcourt, Charles, architect, *see* Masters, Charles Harcourt

Harcourt, Lord, 142

Hardenhuish, near Chippenham, St. Nicholas, 143

Harington, Sir John, 44, 45

Hart, Emma (afterwards Lady Hamilton), 81

'Harvey Block', High Street, 33

Harvey family, masons and architects, 99, 118, 136

Hastings, Lady Margaret, 61
Hawarden, Lady, 96
Hay Hill Baptist Church, 31, 82, 142
Henrietta Street, 80, 137
Herschel, William, musician and astronomer, 89
Hetling House (now Abbey Church House), 27
High Street, 27
Hilliard, Dr. and Mrs., 54
Hinton Charterhouse, Somerset, St. John Baptist, 138
Hippesley, John, actor, 126
Hoare, Prince, sculptor, 99
Hoare, William, painter, 56, 89
Hobbs, John, timber merchant and developer, 141
Holburne of Menstrie Museum (formerly Sydney Hotel), 65, **71**, 137, 140, 141: *71*
Holland, Alfred, developer, 63
Holy Trinity, Combe Down, 138
Holy Trinity (formerly St. Paul), Monmouth Street, 31, **71–2**, 82, 142: *72*
Hot Bath, 27, **72**, 139, 143: *72*
Humphrey Clinker, 58
Hunstrete House, Somerset, 96
Huntingdon, Selina, Countess of, 60–1; Chapel **59–61**: *60*; Connexion, 63
Hutchins, John, plasterer, 80

Irvingite Church, Guinea Lane, 139

Jackson, Sir Thomas, architect, 48
James II, 16
Jay, Rev. William, 63
Jelly, Thomas, builder and architect, 68, 76, 112, 121, 126, 136, **139**, 140
Jenkins, Rev. William, architect, 130
John Street, 135
Johnson, Nicholas, carver, 48
Johnstone Street, 80
Jolly's, Milsom Street, 82
Jones, Inigo, architect, 68
Jones, Richard, clerk of works and architect, 68, 92–6, 123

Kelston Park, near Bath, 143
Kemble, Rev. Charles, 47
Kennet and Avon Canal, 13, **72–4**: *73*
Kennet and Avon Canal Association (later Trust), 74

Kensington Chapel, London Road, **76**, 140: *74*
Kensington Place, London Road, 140
Kent, Duchess of, 86
Killigrew, William, architect, 28, 54, **139**
King, Oliver, Bishop of Bath, 41, 43, 44, 45
King Edward's School, Broad Street, **76**, 139: *75*
King's Bath, 21, 52, 72, 99, 100, 106
Kingsmead Square, 141
Kingston Baths, 139
Kingston Deverill, Wiltshire, St. Mary, 140
Kingswood School, 31, 112, 142

Ladymead, 137
Lansdown Crescent, 20, 54, **76–8**, 123, 140: *76, 78, 79*
Lansdown Place East and West, 76
Lansdown Proprietary College, 112
Laura Chapel, Henrietta Street, 137
Laura Place, 65, **80**, 137: *80*
Leland, John, 27, 41, 45
Lightoler (or Lightholder), Thomas, architect, 68, 88–9, 136
Lilliput Alley, 103
Linley, Elizabeth Ann (later Mrs. R. B. Sheridan), 81
Linley, Thomas, musician, 80
Linley House, Pierrepont Place, **80–1**: *81*
Liverpool, Exchange, 30, 143; St. George's Hall, 138
Livingstone, David, 14
Llandaff Cathedral, 143
Lloyds Bank, Milsom Street and George Street, 84, 142
Lodge Style, Combe Down, **81–2**: *81*
London: Cavendish Square, 142; Grosvenor and Harley estates, 142; Grosvenor Square, 142; hotels, 63; Jesuit Church, Farm Street, 119; Old Burlington Street, 142; Reform Club, 105; St. Pancras Station, 67
'Londonderry', Kingsmead Square, *see* Rosewell House
Loudon, J. C., Landscape gardener, 57
Lowder, John, architect, 136

Lower Borough Walls, 27
Lucas Bath, 106
Lyncombe Hill, 11

Malcolm, J. P., quoted, 86
Malmesbury Abbey, 138
Man, Isle of, 'The Nunnery', 141
Mannasseh, Leonard, architect, 33
Manners, George Philip, architect, 31, 47, 54–5, 57, 86, 111, 118, 138, **139–40**, 141
'Manvers Arms,' 109
Manvers Street, 67, 108; Baptist Chapel, 31, 72, **82**, 142: *82*
Margaret Chapel, 143
Market, 11, 27, 70
Marlborough Buildings, 22, 110, 137
Marston Bigott, near Frome, St. Leonard, 137
Mary of Modena, Queen, 28, 61
Masters, Charles Harcourt, surveyor and architect, 71, 132, 137, 139, **140**
Matthews, Major, 81
Matthyssens, sculptor, 111
Mewès and Davis, architects, 63
Midland Railway, 67; station (Green Park), **67**, 72: *67*
Midsomer Norton, Somerset, St. John Baptist, 141
Miller, Sanderson, architect, 123
Milsom, Daniel, wine cooper and developer, 124
Milsom Street, 17, 82, 124, 136, 139
Mineral Water Hospital, *see* Royal Mineral Water Hospital
Montague, Sir Henry, 47
Montague, James, Bishop of Bath and Wells, 45, 47; tomb, 47
Moravian Chapel, Charlotte Street, *see* Christian Science Church
Moravian Chapel, Coronation Avenue, 58
Morris, Roger, architect, 96

Nash, Richard 'Beau', 12, 14, 15, 17, 28, 52–3, 86, 110; house, 52–3; memorial, 48; statue, 21, 99
National Trust, 51
National Westminster Bank, Milsom Street and George Street, **82–3**, 142: *82*
Nattes, John C., artist, 47

Nelson, Lord, 9, 14
Nelson, Robert, 54
New Bank, 136
New Private Baths, 52, 99, 137
New Sydney Place, *see* Sydney Place
Norfolk Crescent, **84**, 130, 140, 141: *83, 84*
Norfolk, Duke of, 84
North Gate, 27
North Parade (originally Grand Parade), 31, **84–5**, 143
North Parade Bridge, 9
Northgate Street, 27
Northumberland Buildings, Wood Street, **85**, 125, 137: *86*
Norton Malreward, Somerset, Holy Trinity, 142

Obelisks, **86–7**: *87*
Octagon Chapel, Milsom Street, 68, **88–9**: *88*
Old Bridge, 108
Oliver, Dr. William, 103, 111
Orange Grove, 43, 86, **90**: *89*; Obelisk, 86: *87*
Orange, Prince of, 86
Orchard Street, 27
Ordish, F., architect, 67
Ottawa, Canada, Dominion Parliament Buildings, 142
Oxford, Methodist Chapel, New Inn Hall Street, 130
Oxford Row, 130

Page, Samuel, and Philip Flood, architects, 31, 91
Palladian Bridge, *see* Prior Park
Palladio, Andrea, 98
Palmer, John, architect, 30, 61, 68, 76–8, 84, 98–9, 111, 112, 121, 126–7, 136, 138, 139, **140**; memorial, 121
Palmer, John, brewer and chandler, 126, 140
Palmer, John, jnr., postal reformer, 140
Palmer, Thomas, glazier, 139, 140
Parade Gardens, 22
Paragon, 20, 60, **90–1**, 136: *90*
Park Street, 17, 141
Partis, Rev. Fletcher, 91
Partis College, 31, **91**: *91*
Paty, Thomas, architect, 68, 136

Paulton, Somerset, Holy Trinity, 141
Pepys, Samuel, 14, 17
Percy Chapel, Charlotte Street, *see* Elim Chapel
Percy Place, London Road, 63, 140
Phipps, Charles John, architect, 127–8
Pierrepont Place, 80
Pierrepont Street, 14, 67, 80, 85, 108
Pinch, John, the elder, architect, 30, 56, 80, 84, 116–17, 118, 119–20, 125, 140, **141**
Pinch, John, the younger, architect, 71, 103, 119–20, **141**
Pinch, William, builder, 92
'Pinch's Folly', Bathwick Street, **92**: *92*
Pitman, Sir Isaac, 13, 14
Plura, Mr., 'statuary', 76
Plymouth, Guildhall, 138
Police station, 115
Poor House, Milsom Street, 124
Pope, Alexander, 9, 14, 17, 24, 86
Popham, Francis, 96
Post Office, 33
Prior Park, 14, 28, 30, **92–6**, 103, 138, 143: *93, 94, 95*; Palladian Bridge, 24, 96: *93*; St. Paul's Church, 96, **118**: *119*
Prison, Grove Street, **96–7**, 98, 136: *96*; Twerton, 139
Pulteney family, arms, 66
Pulteney, Frances, 80, 97
Pulteney, Henrietta Laura, Countess of Bath, 80
Pulteney, William, Earl of Bath, 97
Pulteney, Sir William Johnstone, 80, 96, 97, 98
Pulteney Bridge, 9, 30, 80, 96, **97–8**, 136: *97*
Pulteney Street, *see* Great Pulteney Street
Pump Room, 17, 20, 21, 31, 33, 51, **98–100**, 136, 137, 140: *23, 98, 99, 100*; first Pump Room, 28, 99, 100

Queen Square, 30, 65, **100–3**, 109, 112, 141, 143: *29, 102, 103*; Obelisk, 86, 103: *87*
Queen Square Station (later Green Park Station), 67
Queen's Bath, 99

Queen's Parade, 49
Queensberry, Duchess of, 14
Quiet Street, 52, 138

Raby Place, Bathwick, 125, 141
Radstock, Somerset, St. Nicholas, 142
Rebecca Fountain, **105**: *105*
Redhill, Somerset, Christ Church, 142
Register Office, Charlotte Street (formerly Bath Savings Bank), **105**: *105*
Rennie, John, engineer, 72
Richardson, Sir Albert, architect, 51
Rivers Street, 143
Roman Baths, 16, 21, 27, **105–6**, 137: *16*
Rome, Colosseum, compared with Circus, 58
Rosewell, Thomas, 107
Rosewell House, Kingsmead Square, **106–7**, 141: *107*
Rotork factory, 33
Royal Crescent, 14, 15, 19, 30, 31, 55, 90, **109–10**, 143: *19, 108, 109, 110*
Royal Hotel, **108–9**: *108*
Royal Mineral Water Hospital (now Royal National Hospital for Rheumatic Diseases), 103, **110–11**, 126, 140, 143: *111*
Royal School, 31, **111–12**, 142: *112*
Russel Street, 48, 143

St. Alphege, Oldfield Park, 33
St. Andrew, 110
St. James, 27, 121, 139, 140
St. James's Parade, **112**, 139, 140: *113*
St. James's Square, **112–14**, 140: *114*
St. James's Street South, 139
St. John, South Parade, 57, **114–15**: *114*
St. John the Evangelist, Weston, Bath, 137
St. John's Court, Sawclose, 52, 139
St. John's Gate, 135
St. John's Hospital, 27, 29, 139; chapel, 139
St. Mark, Lyncombe, 118
St. Mary Bathwick, 31, **116–17**, 119, 120, 138, 141: *115, 116*
St. Mary de Stalles, 27

St. Mary Magdalene, Langridge, Bath, 137
St. Mary within the Walls, North Gate, 27, 76, 96
St. Mary's Buildings, Wells Road, **117–18**, 125: *117*
St. Mary's Chapel, Queen Square, 71–2, 88–9, 143
St. Matthew, Widcombe, 137, 140
St. Michael, Broad Street, 31, 71, 89, **118**, 139: *118*; medieval church (St. Michael-extra-Muros), 118
St. Michael Within, West Gate, 27
St. Michael's Church House, Walcot Street, 132: *130*
St. Paul, Monmouth Street, *see* Holy Trinity
St. Paul, Prior Park, 96, **118–19**: *119*
St. Peter, Lower Bristol Road, 137
St. Saviour, Larkhall, 76, **119–20**, 137, 141: *120*
St. Stephen, Lansdown, 31, **120–1**, 142: *120*
St. Swithin, Walcot, 76, **121**, 139, 140: *121*; cemetery chapel, 57–8: *57*
St. Winifred's Quarry, Combe Down (now Lodge Style), **81–2**: *81*
SS. Peter and Paul, Combe Down, 33
Salisbury, Cathedral, 118; General Infirmary, 143
Saracen's Head, Broad Street, 28, 90, **121–3**: *121*
Sawclose, 127
Scoles, Joseph John, architect, 118–19
Scott, Sir (George) Gilbert, architect, 47, 110, 136, 137
Scott, Sir Giles Gilbert, architect, 33
Sedding, John Dando, architect and craftsman, 120
Seddon, John Pollard, architect, 82
Seymour Street, 140
Sham Castle, 20, 105, **123**: *122*
Sheffield, Methodist Chapel, Carver Street, 130
Sheridan, Richard Brinsley, dramatist, 9, 81
Shipham, Somerset, St. Leonard, 142
Sion Hill Place, 141
Snell, Henry Saxon, architect, 82
Soane, Sir John, architect, 137

Somerset and Dorset Railway, 67
Somerset Place, 56, 68, 76, 78, **123–4**, 138: *76, 122*
Somersetshire Buildings, Milsom Street, **124–5**, 137: *124*
South Gate, 27
South Parade, 31, **84–5**, 143: *85*
Southgate Street, 27
Spa Station, *see* Great Western Railway
Stall Street, 27
Standlynch (later Trafalgar) House, Wiltshire, 143
Stent, F. W., architect, 142
Strahan, John, architect, 28, 53, 106–7, 127, **141**
Stratton-on-the-Fosse, Somerset, Christ Church, 141
Street, George Edmund, architect, 117, 136, 138
Street, William, banker, 89
Stukeley, William, draughtsman, 28
Sul-Minerva, 12, 20
Sussex, Duke of, 64
Sydney Gardens (pleasure gardens), 68, 71, 125
Sydney Hotel (Sydney House), *see* Holburne of Menstrie Museum
Sydney Place, 71, 117, **125**, 137, 141: *123, 125*

Terrace Walk, 27, 90, 103, **125–6**, 143: *126*
Thayer, Humphrey, developer, 84, 143
Theatre, Borough Walls, 110, 126
Theatre (later Theatre Royal), Orchard Street, 64, 126, 139, 140
Theatre, Terrace Walk ('Mr. Simpson's Theatre'), 126
Theatre Royal, Beaufort Square and Sawclose, 53, **126–8**, 140: *127, 128*
Thomas, John, 96
Thomas Street (later St. James's Parade), 112
Thomson, Alexander 'Greek', architect, 54
Thrale, Mrs. (later Mrs. Piozzi), 9, 64, 89
Timber Green (later Sawclose), 27
Tompion, Thomas, clockmaker, 21, 100
Tottenham, Rev. Edward, 76

Tours, John of, *see* Villula, John de
Trim, George, developer, 126
Trim Bridge, 135: *25*
Trim Street, 14, 28, 135
Trowbridge, Market House, 137
Trubshaw, Charles, architect, 63
Tufnell, Samuel, sculptor, 47
Twerton House, 137

Unitarian Church, Trim Street, 140
United Hospital, Beau Street, 140, 141
University of Bath, 15
Uphill, Somerset, St. Nicholas, 142
Upper Borough Walls, 27

Vane family, arms, 125
Vertue, Robert and William, masons, 44
Victoria, Princess, 86
Victoria Park, 109, 137; Obelisk, 86, 139: *86*
Villula, John de (otherwise John of Tours), Bishop of Bath, 41, 42, 43
Voysey, Charles Francis Annesley, architect, 81–2, 136

Wade, General (later Field-Marshal) George, 47, 48, 128; House, Abbey Churchyard, **128–30**, 139: *129*
Wade's Passage (Wade's Alley), 128
Walcot Methodist Chapel, **130**: *130*
Walcot Schools, Guinea Lane, 31, 142
Walcot Street, 20, 91, 121, **130–2**: *130, 131*
Wallinger, Rev. J. B., 64
Walpole, Horace, 60–1, 81
Warburton, Mrs., 96
Webster, Captain, 28
Wesley, John, 60–1, 112
West Gate, 27
Western Dispensary, Albion Place, 62
Westgate Buildings, 27
Westgate Street, 27, 28
Westminster Abbey, Henry VII's Chapel, 44
Weston-super-Mare, Emmanuel Church, 140
Weymouth House, 139
Whitefield, George, 60–1

Widcombe, 24, 133

Widcombe Crescent, **132–3**, 140: *132, 134*

Widcombe Hill, 11

Widcombe Manor House, **133–5**, 139: *133*

Widcombe Terrace, **132–3**, 140: *132*

Wilkins, William, architect, 31, 64, 136

Willcox, William John, architect, 31, 71–2, 82, 120, **142**

Wilson, James, architect, 31, 56–8, 71–2, 111–12, 120–1, **142**

Wilson, J. B., architect, 71–2, 142

Wilton, Wiltshire, Palladian Bridge, 96

Windsor, St. George's Chapel, 44, 45

Winifred's Dale, 141

Wolfe, General, 14; House, Trim Street, 14, **135**: *25*

Wood, John, the elder, architect, 12–13, 28–30, 58–9, 64–5, 71, 76, 80, 84–5, 86, 88, 92–6, 100–3, 110–11, 121, 126, **142–3**; *Essay*, 45, 143; quoted, 68, 99, 118, 130–1, 141

Wood, John, the younger, architect, 30, 48–9, 55, 65, 68, 72, 109–10, **143**

Woodforde, 'Parson', 89

Younghusband, Francis, 20

ECCE QUAM BONUM ^ IUCUNDUM ~~ECCE~~
ET QUAM EST